ASCENSION

The Accelerated Path
into the New Millennium

BY
BETSY-MORGAN COFFMAN

Foreword by Tony Stubbs
Author of
An Ascension Handbook
and Co-author of
The Divine Blueprint

Gabriel Light Publishing

Ascension
The Accelerated Path
into the New Millennium
by
Betsy-Morgan Coffman

Published in 2009
Copyright © 2009 by Betsy-Morgan Coffman

Published by
GABRIEL LIGHT PUBLISHING
6704 CYPRESS POINT WAY
ALBUQUERQUE, NM 87111
VOICE: (505) 275-4746
E-MAIL: askbetsymorgan@yahoo.com
WEBSITE: www.askbetsymorgan.com

Printed in the United States of America
ISBN-13 978-0-9821769-1-7

Library of Congress Cataloging in Publication Data
Library of Congress Control Number: 2009925549

Cover design by Diana Massengale, Image Design LLC
Cover photo by Kimberly Lynn Young
Transcription, Layout & Design by Destiny McCune
Edited by Tony Stubbs

Contents

Foreword by Tony Stubbs   iv
Dedication   vii
In Appreciation   viii
Introduction   ix

PART I – ASCENSION
1   Ascension - What Is It; Why Is It Important?   1
2   Signs from the Heart   9
3   Experiences of Awakening   21
4   How to Prepare for Ascension   35
5   What Will Occur for Planet Earth   41
6   Exercises   51
    a) Cleansing
    b) Manifestation
    c) De-stressing
    d) Ascension
7   Angels Among You   65

PART II – THE GIFT OF THE SHIFT
8   Focus and Frequency   69
9   Earth Predictions and How to Overcome Them   87

PART III – ORION CHANNELS
I Am the Light of the Oneself   103
Akhenaten   115
How to Integrate the New Energy   129
Be Bold in the Light   137

PART IV – RESOURCES   146

Foreword

Traditionally, the only way to ascend into the realms of unconditional love and bliss is to leave your body behind and cross over. Then you get to spend eternity on the soul plane unless you-the-soul opt to incarnate again. But as of the Harmonic Convergence in August 1987, that all changed.

The catalyst for this was Gaia, the consciousness of planet Earth, who was not a happy camper. She'd been pummeled by two world wars as human egos duked it out, with no regard for her. Her life blood, oil, was being pumped out of her body at an alarming rate. And the final straw was 40 years of above-ground and below-ground nuclear testing, not to mention unbridled poisoning of her lakes, rivers and oceans, which she had so generously shared with us to enjoy. Not surprising that after centuries of abuse, Gaia was ticked off…and vowed to do something drastic, such as inviting a huge asteroid to slam into her body, so her body could "die" and she could leave for other dimensions.

She did offer humanity an alternative, however. She gave us 25 years to get our act together, which takes us to the year 2012. Her plan is to ascend in 2012, and those of us who are ready will go with her. Those who are not ready will cross over and reincarnate on a new planet whose consciousness is much younger than that of Gaia, and ready to play host to those souls who choose to incarnate on her to finish out their cycle of lifetimes.

So what is this "ascension"? In 1991, my first book, *AHH*, offered a brief roadmap, which served as a guide to the terrain. But things have evolved in the almost two decades since then, and many new perspectives are coming out, courtesy of dedicated beings in the higher dimensions, such as Orion and Akhenaten, and gifted channels such as Betsy.

Being the book's editor gave me an outstanding opportunity to "get inside the material," which I found both educational and inspirational. These pages offer invaluable explanations of what we can expect over the next few years as waves of energy of ever-increasing frequency sweep across the planet. Actually it's more accurate to say, "as the planet moves through ever more highly charged regions of space." And the explanations go a long way to dispel any fear we may have about what we'll encounter along the way.

In addition to educating us, Orion and Akhenaten express their profound gratitude for our courage in showing up as lightworkers for the ascension of a planet with the densest energy ever known in the cosmos…a feat that's never been done before. So we are writing our script as we go and adjusting to massive energy waves along the way. To this end, they flood these pages with inspiration and encouragement. They also promise to show up in your space as you read, but for that, they need your permission, so to be sure to invite them in.

In summary, I encourage you to set aside several hours of uninterrupted time, and just lose yourself in this book. Reading something of this caliber is not a pastime but an experience, and deserves your undivided attention. Really get into the visualizations and let them take you where your soul wills. Or you may read it once quickly to survey the terrain, and then several times more for thorough exploration. Either way, this is not a book you will read just once. You could even just open a page "at random," knowing you will read the passage that's exactly what you need at that moment.

However you use it, you will not be disappointed by this treasure trove of truth, love, wisdom and compassion.

Tony Stubbs, author of *An Ascension Handbook*

Dedication

For
Aidan Ocean and Shae Ryan,
my grandchildren,
a gift from my daughter, Kimberly

* * *

For
Angelina,
Destiny's grandchild,
a gift from her daughter, Cristi

In Appreciation

I am richly blessed with many friends and family who have supported me in my journey, and I want to thank you all. My life and this book would not be the same without you.

I want to include Tony Stubbs, friend, editor, and author of his own books, for writing the foreword, and for assisting me in more ways than he knows.

I want to thank Shirley MacLaine for her time given in reading my manuscript and all support offered. Thank you, Shirley.

I would like to include a hug of "thanks!" to the many, many teachers who have touched me, and have contributed to the quality of my life and to this book.

I want to thank all my beloved students who show me daily the extent of their love for me and this work. Your love alone heals me daily and helps to lift my world. Can you just imagine what it is doing for our planet? Thank you, thank you for your amazing courage, willingness and dedication. I love you!

Most of all, I wish to thank Orion—my teacher... my friend.

Introduction

The ascension is the foundation of Orion's gift. When Orion first came in to talk to me in 1992, he shared his intention to work with human beings, first in letting all of us know there are star beings who are available to us, who want to help us, and who love us and will help us when invited.

Secondly, Orion wants us to know he will help each one of us lift our frequency in order to connect with star beings for the purpose of channeling wisdom, light, love and healing when invited.

The purpose of the ascension is to lift frequency and to live a life that demonstrates compassion, peace, patience and joy, a life with less anger, grief, blame, shame and sadness. We begin to live consciously from love.

One of the ways Orion works with us is through this process called ascension. The ascension may be accomplished in a very simple exercise that only takes three to five minutes. Or you may spend as long as ten or fifteen minutes in this ascension exercise if you like, but Orion makes it very clear that it is more important to do the ascension exercise one to three times a day than it is to do it only every now and then for 15 minutes or longer.

What happens during the ascension exercise is a kind of energetic technology, based on the fact we are all connected to love and to each other through a matrix of light, and that the highest frequency wins, or lifts lower frequency.

We actually set an intention into motion through thought energy. We have a kind of kingdom, which is called consciousness. Our kingdom is actually our energy field, or our aura, and through a conscious intention request, we can command the aura to lift in frequency with Orion's help. It will actually lift so high that we can connect with our soul's path and plan.

If we are in error in our thinking, actions or emotions, through a higher healed intention and help through this "assistance program" called ascension, we can be lifted in our frequency and actually connect with our soul plan.

When we make that connection with the intention for healing, we simply ask that we integrate with our soul's plan. During the process of ascension, this actually occurs, and we energetically connect with our soul's plan. While that is occurring, all negativities begin to dissolve.

We allow ourselves, again through intention, asking for divine help, and help from the Orion technology, to release negative thought patterns, to allow them to be dissolved, to allow all imbalanced emotions to come into harmony, and to allow physical healings to take place in our body. We affirm that it is God's will that we prosper and are happy, and we let go of a false belief that we need to suffer in order to grow. We ask for a healed perception.

We align with the plan of our soul to manifest our highest destiny. We align with the plan of God that *His will be done*, which is to be happy and to prosper. We do not need to know *how* this happens, but simply be willing to do the exercise.

xii

———

Part I

ASCENSION

* * *

"Ascension is the lifting of energy. This is a process and a destiny of human beings, for this lifting of energy we call ascension is quite simply evolution."

* * *

1

Ascension - What Is It; Why Is It Important?

Greetings, beloveds. We are pleased to make your acquaintance. We say "to make your acquaintance" for every day, you are new as you allow yourselves to move with the energies rather than resist them. This movement with the higher frequencies allows you to enjoy greater health and a sense of well being.

This sense of trust is now finding itself coupled with an element of compassion, for as you flow with life, this that is true about you begins to surface. This is the effect of the ascension.

The ascension is the subject we would like to discuss. Let us start with a definition. Ascension is the lifting of energy. This is a process and a destiny of human beings, for this lifting of energy we call ascension is quite simply *evolution*.

It has been going on for a long time, but the reason it has come into your awareness now is because you as a species have finally ascended, or risen, to a level of spiritual equivalency where you are simply aware of it. The fact that it is a natural process may be the part that is new to you. The fact that it is ongoing also may be new to you.

The truth about ascension is that it has escalated recently and temporarily. The lifting of frequency for the purpose of evolving the human species and the planet Earth will be on a speedup program until 2012, at which time there will be an integration period, an enhancement of this energetic process completing itself in 2016. At 2016, you will then be able to see the measurable effects of increasing vibration of energy.

This process called "ascension" that is happening to you right now is allowing you to release discord of all nature, the focal point being emotional blockages, pain, and attachments to the past. Let us simply call this, for a phrase, negative emotions, which prevent you from lifting in ascension. Lifting in ascension could be called moving forward into your light body.

We wish to explain a few other words so you have a vocabulary where there is consensus or agreement of what these words mean, so that we can continue our discussion. Let us say that consciousness is "a set of beliefs that creates your reality." Let us say that dimension is a state of consciousness or awareness. The higher your frequency, the higher your state of consciousness or awareness.

Therefore, through the process of ascension, you heal mis-beliefs, thus lifting consciousness. When consciousness or awareness vibrates at a higher frequency, you become available to higher dimensions.

We would like to clarify here that dimensions just are. The higher dimensions are not being created necessarily by your new awareness of them. They are already here. They are rather a state of awareness you are now in harmony with.

You might imagine a hot air balloon rising, and as it rises, it catches the wind that might be blowing east or west, north or south at different levels of altitude. The wind that is blowing is a constant, but as the balloon lifts higher and higher, it becomes aware of the different directions of movement.

Your energy body has sufficiently ascended to where you are now aware and integrating with the higher dimensions. You have actually moved out of the third dimension and are beginning to integrate with the fifth dimension.

We would like at this time to explain the difference between the third, fourth and fifth dimensions of awareness. Each dimension is basically different because of frequency. The third dimension, where humanity used to live, was defined by states of polarity and a sense of separation promoted by the ego mind.

Dimension four is more of a dimension of transition. This is where you move through as you are releasing the emotional blockages. As negative emotional blockages are released, through the lifting of energy, you essentially lighten up and go higher, finding yourself finally on the fifth dimension. This state of awareness will mirror itself as a happier physical reality. You will not leave the planet earth, although it will simply appear to you as a happier and healthier place of existence.

Not all human beings will ascend to the fifth dimension. It is always a choice by the individual. Free will is honored everywhere in the universe. Although every human being will eventually evolve, everyone has a right to choose how quickly this is done for them.

When you "arrive" on the fifth dimension, you will become aware of greater harmony, unity and compassion among human beings. The human beings who live in the fifth dimension will have at their core similar values, especially humanitarian service and love for all.

This does not mean you will lose your sense of being an individual. You will simply be learning higher lessons about cooperation. You will still be creative, unique and very interested in finding compatible romantic relationships and somewhat invested in self-actualization, but less competitive, less in a rush to get somewhere else other than where and who you are right now.

You will be more aware that all is well in the moment. You will be aware that even those people who are antagonistic to you are serving you as teachers and you will experience a level of gratitude for the lesson. You will also be living with a greater state of inner peace and well being.

Some of you will begin to develop gifts of spirit. This is because, again, of frequency. As you know, everything is energy and the only thing that separates the perception of what the energy looks like is the frequency at which that energy vibrates and the agreement that is given to it.

The agreement in the fifth dimension is that your chakras will be more open and communicating with the divine, and thus receptive to the higher laws of God rather than the third-dimensional laws of man. Therefore, you will be more creative.

As you think and feel, it will occur in the physical more quickly. Your heart's passions will become manifested in a physical reality.

Some of you will then experience levitation, relocation, energetic healing, complete psychic awareness, and your artistic expression will be phenomenal. Your hearing, seeing and tasting will be more acute.

With the increased frequencies, there will be an awakening of the DNA. Some of you know there is a double strand of DNA that is awakened in the third-dimensional human. As an individual lifts through the fourth dimension and releases emotional pain and limited belief systems, that individual becomes more available to the awakening of more DNA. This basically awakens more of your brain cells and makes you a more intelligent being.

Universal love or God has arranged that your mind open in harmony with your heart so you do not extinct yourselves. Your mind could not open faster than your heart. This that is ascension opens the heart first, releases blockages, activates DNA, and then opens new brain matter. You will feel an exquisite freedom.

We hope this begins to make sense to you and will not go into greater detail, but encourage you to trust the process. Let us repeat and simplify what this process is. The process always begins with willingness to love. As you are willing to love yourself and others, the frequency of compassion and the frequency of trust build in you, and your energy body lightens up. This is ascension.

We who come from another universe are simply more ascended than you. We have more capabilities accessible to us than you and are eager and excited to share this good news with you now. The reason we can share it with you now is because you as a species have evolved enough to hear it. This information was always here, but you were not. Not all human beings are ascending at the same rate.

There is a universal law called "entrainment"—the higher frequency wins or lifts the lower frequency. If you are reading this book, you are a high frequency being and can lift other beings of light (human beings).

It is important, however, to keep your energy field cleansed, to give to yourself good self-care, physical and emotional, to remember to be patient with those who are slow, but do not try to rescue them. Stay in the light. When a human being is ready, they will come into the light using their free will correctly. Rescuing others may tend to contaminate you, and you will grow weary. It is like going into quicksand, and you may not have the physical strength or stamina to get out before you are pulled down. Love yourself enough to stay in the light at all times. Know and honor your balance.

Ascension is a high frequency that allows evolution of the human species. Each individual ascends at their own rate. As you ascend, you heal your state of consciousness. This means you change and heal your beliefs and limited thinking. You heal and release emotional pain, distortion and attachment to the past.

You become more available to light, and automatically lift through the fourth dimension into the fifth. Here you will feel lighter, happier, freer and more creative, and some of you will begin to see physically some of us in the higher realms of light.

There are higher dimensions, but most of you will integrate the fifth one in this lifetime. This is not to say you will not become greatly aware of the sixth and seventh, and yes a few of you even the eighth, but we do not see many of you integrating in this lifetime higher than the fifth dimension. The reason for this is that this dimension is beautiful, there is plenty to explore and many, many lessons to learn here. You could spend several lifetimes at the fifth dimension and enjoy it very much.

When you are living in the fifth dimension, you will see in the physical realm of the fifth dimension more beauty and love everywhere. This is because the truth that your consciousness mirrors itself is still in effect.

Your consciousness will be cleansed and purified, and therefore what it is mirroring to you for you to enjoy will simply be more beautiful and harmonious with your higher nature. There are great gifts to behold and enjoy here.

This ascension process is underway and will culminate in 2012 to be enjoyed fully in 2016. Please remember, do not be eager to move along. There is nowhere to go. The greatest lesson is simply learning to be here now in love. If you learn that lesson, you will skim right along as quickly as you would wish to. This we reassure you.

There is an ascension exercise in this book and an ascension exercise CD available to you. At the back of this book, you will find information on how to purchase this CD.

If you do these exercises, you will find you are moving along as quickly as is comfortable for you, because ascension is always accompanied by cleansing. You would not wish to cleanse too quickly. It could feel too abusive to your system. Take your time and *trust, lift* and *love*. Those are the key words to this chapter.

2

Signs from the Heart

There are many signs that so many human beings are not paying attention to. It is not a waste of time for your collective consciousness when you allow yourselves to move with these higher energies, for you are helping the good of the whole.

The world is like a hologram and each of you is a part of it, and as any one of you begins to accept the calling to come home (and that is to the fifth dimension), you help every single human being because you are connected by a matrix of light. Likewise, you are connected to us through the same matrix of light, and who would we be if not your brothers and sisters from the stars, and angels, indeed, from heaven? We are all a part of the one sun-ship.

When we mention there are signs, some of the signs are not physical. Some of the signs come from an inner longing to go home or a feeling that you are a fish out of water. This is the awakening of your higher awareness recognizing it is not home and longing to be there.

This process we call ascension, the lifting of frequency, will provide an avenue or a portal for the reunion of the higher self into a larger portion of its soul awareness.

The invisible signs are encouraging messages of love from us star beings and angels. We are in essence talking to you all the time. It is as if we have a telephone call to you and are on speaker 24/7. We will advise you what to do, where to go, and when to be there. We are always encouraging you with loving acts of kindness, humility, compassion and love.

Some of the human beings are listening and acting, and some are not. Yet we want you who are reading this book to be aware of this truth so you can acknowledge what is going on within you and feel more comfortable and reassured that this is occurring and is not just your imagination ... although your imagination is a wonderful tool for enlightenment.

Dear ones, when you receive an impulse or a thought process that is loving and encouraging, often it comes from us in the higher realms. We have been assigned to you to help you through this process called ascension.

When we have spoken of the fact that some of you will go to the left and some of you will go to the right, we are referring not only to you as individual human beings, but to the ego going to the left and the heart going to the right. This division will happen on many different levels.

Your ego cannot go home with you, for it is the belief in separation and the substantiation of all manifestations of fear. Where we are taking you, there is no such thing as ego.

What we would like this chapter to be about are the signs that come from the heart, which have been directly impressed upon the heart by us, your friends of light in the stars and in the heavens. We would like each one of you reading this book to take some time this day to review or recall experiences you have had in the light that you may not have understood or perhaps even been tempted to not believe were true.

We have come this day to reassure you that all of these miracles and metaphysical experiences were not only real, but came from a higher truth, a more graduated form of expression, a form of expression that needs no physical form at all. Your higher sense perception is growing as you begin to notice the signs that are not physical at all.

We from the higher realms will reach you through your emotions, your imagination, your feelings and the impulse to do good. Allow yourself more and more often to go with the flow of these higher yearnings. As you take action, loving action, you will begin to align yourself physically with the higher frequencies.

You cannot *think* your way into heaven. Heaven is a state of *being*, but you must act upon the impulse to love; then it becomes substantiated in your reality. Reality is but, because of the ego, it makes you believe it is perception. When you let go of the ego, you begin to see and experience what has always been there, which is love itself. You must learn to trust and act upon love for no reason other than love in order to experience that love is everywhere now.

After your reading this chapter, we will begin to come in to you, dear reader, in larger impulses, speaking to you and giving you through impulses and emotional lifting so that you can experience this that we are telling you is real.

We would like for this book to be an experience, an exercise of growing into love, of growing into the kingdom of heaven on earth and not just another book. Please take our invitation to make it real by doing the exercises and activities offered.

The exercise for you to do today would be to love everyone who comes into your physical proximity more fully, with greater forgiveness and compassion.

Please notice that when you start to do this, the portion of your mind called the ego will resist this greatly. It will do this by looking for reasons not to love, reasons to blame, reasons to separate and reasons to persist in drama.

None of this is important because none of it is real. Only love is real. Only the love you give and receive will continue on. So, dear reader, we will escalate our production of frequencies of loving messages moving into your conscious awareness so that you might choose with your own volition to act upon love. Then, according to your readiness and willingness, you will find love everywhere. This will provide for you an encouragement to follow this path.

We will make note here that as you reach this portion of the book, your ego may become greatly activated. You may want to put the book down and find reasons to not believe we are speaking. Be aware that the ego will be on alert at this stage. It will recognize that it is, in a sense, dying, and it is dying to the old. You must die in order to be born again. This is what the Bible meant.

There are two reasons why the ego will be on alert. One is because of the immense energy coming forth from the frequency of these words. And two, we are telling you how you can, in essence, destroy the ego.

That directive to destroy the ego would be to choose to stop looking at drama. The only reason you look at the drama in your life is you continue to have a belief that it serves you somehow, that it has value. It is not valuable. It only continues the illusion.

Whatever you find value in, you will continue. Give yourself the chance to find value in love alone … and we are showing you how to do that.

Exercise for Today

Exercise one, step one: Whenever anyone walks into your physical existence, smile at them and say these words: Hello, it's nice to see you. How are you today?

Two, allow yourself to smile and choose to radiate holy energy to your friend as they answer your question.

Three, remember that they may respond from their drama and their belief in their drama. While they talk to you, continue to hold the space of love.

Four, choose to believe that love will heal all fear. This frequency will be moving into their auric field, and they will be receiving it according to their willingness and readiness to receive unconditional love at that moment.

Five, silently ask for an angel to cleanse your aura of any negative energies you might have brought in, and respond to their communication in a loving manner.

Choose to not give any agreement to negativity, but to find a way to uplift all communication. In this way, you can neutralize negative effects and even heighten positive ones.

When the conversation is complete, end your communication with a loving remark such as, "It was wonderful to see you," "I feel better for having been with you," and, "I hope you do too." When you state this, you automatically allow true reality to weave into your auric field. You can actually change reality as you state it into being.

Perhaps you were not truly excited to see them, but as you state it, your body/mind will look for any piece that was true and expand it, creating love in the place of fear.

As you depart, think to yourself, *Go in love.*

Finally, if there is any thought in you at all that thinks you feel you have absorbed negativity, ask for a final cleansing. Give thanks that you could be of service, and love and appreciate yourself more deeply.

In truth, you are emissaries of light, and you have come at this time in recognition that the greatest service you can bring to yourself and to others is the gift of unconditional love.

In time, this seemingly simple conversation will become an automatic response to everyone you meet...and the ego's hold on you will lessen.

At different times throughout your day, you find the ego activated, such as when you are in traffic, standing too long in lines or in crowds of people. These seem to be the times when the ego wants you to feel you are better than everyone else and should have certain advantages. At times like this, it so good to have a sense of humor. When you notice yourself judging others, laugh at the unconscious process of the mind, and choose again.

Exercise two, step one: Stop and breathe and laugh. Take the thought, *Oops, I have believed in the illusion again. It's okay. I will always have another chance to self-correct. I love myself infinitely, and so does God. This situation is not even really happening. I live in an ocean of love and loving responses. I choose to feel love now, for love is who I am.*

Bring in a cleansing angel to cleanse all of the negative out of your auric field and your body/mind. Allow yourself to feel the wonderful pink aura of love moving through every cell of your being and bringing you into harmony with the God-self. Let this radiance move out into everyone you see until it fills the entire building.

Ask for 10,000 angels to come in and cleanse the building to unify all consciousness at the highest level possible. Ask for Archangel Michael to cut the cords of negativity so only love remains.

Feel a pull of pure white and golden light coming in from your top chakra all the way down through your spine and radiating out through every cell of your body.

Take this thought, *I choose to bless the world. I am a blessing as I come from love and forgiveness. I love and forgive everyone, beginning with myself.* And then choose to smile. Smile at anyone who comes forward.

Be patient. Give up your place in line. Be kind. You will see what will happen is your action of love will become contagious, and you will begin to bring harmony into a field of chaos.

You have done your service for the day, and it only took a few seconds. We thank you for this, our beloved angel of light. If only 1,000 of you did this on the planet daily, the world could be saved in 1,000 days. And this is possible.

Allow yourself to notice at this time that you may be wondering where we are in assisting you from higher realms. We mentioned giving you spiritual signs of love. We want you to know we are the energy of love behind all of your actions. We are the energy of cleansing, healing, protection and forgiveness. We are the energy of permission to love yourself.

All it takes to activate this energy is to *choose* to feel it and see it as valuable. If you choose now to change your life by listening and acting upon the signs of love, you will move into higher awareness more quickly than you might believe.

You will recognize you are living in a state of higher awareness when you laugh more than you complain, when you feel freer more often than you worry, and when life begins to manifest prosperity of every good thing more than the deterioration of the essentials of life.

Your prosperity will come to you through healed relationships, a healed body, mind and spirit, a full pocketbook and a peaceful balanced connection to source. You will truly be experiencing the riches of life.

***

Channeling is one of the most interesting and immediate connections to our messages to you. Up to this point, we have been talking about subtle and unconscious promotion of love through the waves of energy we promote into your body/mind. If you choose to, you can connect with us consciously through a technique called channeling.

Channeling is the process of experiencing truth by connecting to beings of light from higher realms. We will speak words that are in alignment with your vocabulary and your passion in order to enhance the quality of your life. We are happy to give you guidance, healing and at times even predictions. The predictions are given only so that you can redirect your actions to be in alignment with a happier outcome.

If you are interested in learning more about channeling, please take a moment to look at the information on resources for channelers and teachers of channeling on page 146. Find the channeling teacher you align with, and simply contact them for more information.

It is possible for you to learn to channel in one weekend. These people have all been approved by the Orion technologies and have been specifically taught by me, Orion.

When you learn to channel with one of them, you will align with my light, with your star being friends, with your home planet, and with your specific angels and channeling guides who will help you live as happy a life as possible.

Channeling is basically the process of integrating higher energy and will help you to transmute negativity so you can enter into the new kingdom of Heaven more easily and sooner. Channeling a being of light brings our frequency into your auric field.

The ascension process itself includes awakening the DNA in your cellular structure. Approximately 97 percent of your cells appear to be empty space, but we tell you it is not empty space. It is consciousness—

consciousness that is waiting to be reawakened through frequency.

As you channel love and light from the higher realms, you begin to reawaken your DNA, thus living from higher truths and activating your unique spiritual gifts.

This is, quite simply, an incredibly joyful life. This is not to say you will stop suffering if you still want to suffer, but it will become very obvious to you that you have a choice. You will see it is needless to suffer and will be much more encouraged to choose a path of love and service.

Channeling a being of light can help you in many ways: (1) It can increase longevity, if you are interested in that, and (2) It attracts prosperity, spiritual peace of mind and spiritual awakening.

You might say these are side-effects of frequency. Your spiritual tensile strength will grow so you will be more prepared to move into this new millennium.

We encourage all of you who are interested in channeling to investigate this path further. As far as we are concerned, this is the quickest path to ascension and thus enlightenment. Once you learn to channel, we would suggest that you do it daily as a spiritual exercise. Ultimately, you will find the culmination of this path spiritual union and freedom.

20

———

ASCENSION

3
Experiences of Awakening

As we began working with Betsy-Morgan in the early 1970s, she had some experiences that changed her life and left her wondering, *What is the truth of the universe?* We are going to share these experiences with you now, dear reader, because many of you will relate to these, and they will give you peace of mind and understanding that life is more than the third dimension. We have been reaching out to you all along.

When Betsy-Morgan was in her early twenties, she was working as a consumer food specialist of the Department of Agriculture in Missouri. Her job necessitated that she would drive for hours at a time from television station to television station in order to promote Missouri agricultural products.

During one particular late evening, when it was close to midnight and Betsy was still en route to Kansas City, Missouri, she noticed a bright light out the left side of her car window. The light seemed to shine directly on her car like a soft flashlight just on her car alone.

At first she thought it was a helicopter and slowed down, but there was no sound. She opened her window and allowed the cool night breeze to blow in and continued to stare at the object. After ten minutes, when the object had not moved and the light was still shining on her vehicle traveling sixty miles an hour down the freeway, she received the thought, *What if this is a spacecraft?*

Being from Missouri, she would not even believe her own thoughts. Of course, this is a thought we prompted to her. We wanted her to begin to be aware of us. She was stubborn though, and laughed at her own thinking. And yet we followed her for a full 35 minutes, during which time we sent to her very high frequency, opening the frontal lobe of her mind for the future communication that was soon to come from us.

She has never forgotten that moment, and only for the first time in this writing are we confirming it was us.

We are the Pleiadians, and we love her and you deeply. We are here to help each one of you through the ascension process.

If you have ever thought you have seen a spacecraft, or how you often term it a flying saucer, chances are you have.

When Betsy-Morgan was in her thirties, she had two lovely children. Her son, Gannon, was born very aware of star beings and our love for you. When he was six years old, he asked his mother if she would help him to connect with a young starling.

Very interested and excited, Betsy-Morgan said, "Yes, of course," and that very day they sat together hand-in-hand and prayed out loud, "Dear friends in the stars, if you can hear us, please know that this young man, Gannon, would like to have a young star being about his age to be his good friend. Would you please come to Gannon and introduce yourself so that the two of you can understand your different cultures and be friends? We're open to meeting you any time. Thank you."

That night, when Betsy-Morgan tucked in her son, she had a strange, almost eerie, feeling. Still, she walked into her own room, turned out the lights and went to sleep. Yet at 2 a.m., she woke, wide awake as if she had never fallen asleep.

She knew immediately she had to go to her son's room. She walked through the dark apartment, not turning on a single light. Getting to her son's room, she placed her hand on the light switch and paused. She stood there a full minute, peering into the darkness, not seeing or hearing a thing.

Still, Betsy-Morgan was very uncomfortable. She felt something other than her son in that room. She felt Gannon's fear, so without turning on the light switch, she lay down on the bottom bunk of his bed, eyes wide open, still listening, waiting. Nothing. So she decided to sleep there the rest of the night, just in case something were to occur, and she fell asleep.

Betsy-Morgan awoke the next morning bright and early to her son tugging on her arm. "Mom, mom, wake up. They came, they came. Why didn't you turn on that light switch? I saw your hand on the light switch. Why didn't you turn it on? I was so scared. They were here. They came to get me. They invited me to go with them."

Betsy-Morgan woke up wide-eyed, bewildered, unbelieving what she had just heard. She asked her son to tell her more, but he was afraid as well. "Mom, they came into my room through the window—a small star being, an alien, and his father. They told me I could go with them, but I couldn't come back. I was afraid they were going to take me against my will. At that moment you walked in, they stood there and looked at you as you looked into the room. I was too scared to speak, but with my mind, I was telling you to turn on the light, but you didn't. I'm so glad you stayed. I think they would have taken me if you hadn't come in. When you laid down on the bed, they left through the window. I don't want them to come back."

At that moment, Gannon looked down and saw on the floor a tuft of wiry, black hair, and he grabbed it and showed it to Betsy-Morgan. "Mom, this was part of the hair that this alien had on him," and he sat down and drew a picture immediately of what the young alien looked like.

Betsy-Morgan recognized her son's fear and the urgency to disconnect. They got down on their knees at that moment and prayed, asking the angels to protect them, especially Gannon, and then sent up a second message: "Dear beings of light in the stars, thank you for hearing our original request. We are too afraid to go through with this. We do not want you to return. Please hear this. In no uncertain terms, do not come back. We ask for angels to cut the connection and only love remain." And they never returned.

Betsy-Morgan contacted Robert Shapiro, of whom you can read more about in the *Sedona* magazine. He channels Zoosh.

Robert brought much peace to Gannon, explaining that he is an advanced spiritual being of light, but his time for service has not come yet, not until he will be in his thirties.

He lovingly told Gannon his job now was to be a little boy, to play with trains and trucks and balls, and just let himself grow up. His opportunity to know star beings would come to him at a later time. This was enough for Gannon, and he slept peacefully through the night.

We want you to know the star beings who came into Gannon's room were advanced, but Gannon was not ready for this level of what he perceived a confrontation. They came only through request and have never returned. Although they felt bothersome at the time, they have respected Gannon and Betsy-Morgan's wishes, and they thank them continuously for that.

This experience for Gannon changed him completely. The light from the star being opened him in such a way that he now moves into the fourth dimension frequently while he sleeps.

He is what you would call a gatekeeper. He is a warrior of light, a protector, and when necessary, he leaves his body at night to assist other human beings to feel secure in staying in the light, to have good boundaries.

Being a gatekeeper is not always comfortable or an easy task. You can physically feel the vibration of the room as if it is an earthquake. You may experience the covers being pulled off your body, the sound of a huge ocean wave crashing against your head.

These are all experiences of the fourth dimension. If you find yourself having any of these, it will help you to be very, very grounded.

Activities to help you be grounded would be physical exercise, eating protein, singing and dancing, hugging other human beings, having a pet, and doing this exercise.

Grounding Exercise

While sitting with your spine erect or standing erect, ask for a grounding angel of light to come in. Gabriel would be a good grounding angel, if you do not know who else to invite. He will always assist.

Allow yourself to imagine light pouring into the top of your head and ask the light to go all the way through your body, through your feet and into the center of the Earth.

Tie a golden cord to the center of the Earth. Ask Gabriel, as well as your guardian angels, to keep you tethered to the Earth plane.

Breathe in three slow, deep breaths. Think to yourself, *I allow myself to ground to Mother Earth. I am grounded by love. I am grounded through my free will of choice, and I am safe. I am grounded now.*

Being grounded in your body and your life will help you when you sleep at night, and you will not experience these disturbing sensations so deeply.

Now you know what is going on, this alone can be comforting. You are serving the light, but you do not need to be uncomfortable in doing so.

Later, in her thirties, Betsy-Morgan was invited to Brazil and had the rare opportunity to visit Mauricio Paniset's home called Enoch. Mauricio Paniset is an exquisite, one-of-a-kind world healer. Although he has passed into the kingdom of Heaven to do his work from a higher realm, he is lovingly remembered by friends and family alike.

Betsy-Morgan was in a group of approximately 20 people late at night when Mauricio introduced all of them to deva spirits who sparkled like fireflies, similar to Tinkerbell in Peter Pan. They were all around, offering great love and the awareness of the love that comes from pets and animals, and how healing and supportive the energy from pets and animals really is.

Then Mauricio invited the group to rest on the huge rocks that were scattered around his estate, and each person lay on those rocks staring into the heavens as different spacecraft came and hovered above the group. This experience lasted about 20 minutes.

Mauricio gathered everyone around and said, "This is a very special experience and happens frequently on my land. I am very accepted by what I call 'my space brothers' and they often put on a show for me so that fellow human beings who are ready to see can live and share the stories of truth—that humans do have a family from the stars who love them, a family who is ready to communicate to them and help them when they are ready to receive their love."

When Betsy-Morgan was in her early forties, I, Orion, came into her life. I came in by impressing my thoughts into her mind in such a conscious way that she actually heard my voice speak aloud saying, "Hello."

We carried on quite a conversation and Betsy-Morgan was willing to follow my dictates, my instructions, in order for her to bring me through the channeled state to literally thousands of people on the Earth plane today. I thank Betsy-Morgan for bringing my light through her vehicle for the purpose of awakening.

I laugh when I share this story about her resistance to believe I was real. Betsy-Morgan is from Missouri and loves to say it is the show-me state. She will not believe anything unless it is shown to her. In order to believe, even though I was talking out loud in her head, she said, "You must show me your presence if you are real."

I spoke to her reassuringly, "Allow yourself to go to the foothills of the Sandia Mountains. Go all the way up Indian School road until you find a National Park. Do this at midnight with a group of friends. Take flashlights and go up into the foothills and meditate under the stars, and I will reveal myself to you. Do this on August 27th."

Betsy-Morgan agreed, and immediately called three willing friends. All four volunteers met that night at ten till midnight, got out of their cars, taking their flashlights, walked up into the foothills, sat under the stars and meditated. Betsy-Morgan had told each one they would see Orion.

At the completion of one hour, I did not show in the physical, but I had left my signature energetically in each one of their energy fields, especially in Betsy-Morgan's and around her particular vehicle—not a spacecraft, but an automobile.

At the end of the hour, the group, disappointed, left the mountain, each one approaching their car. When Betsy-Morgan opened her car door, the alarm went off loud and clear. I played a joke on her, and I had activated her auto alarm system, which had not been activated for four years.

Of course, it startled everyone and probably woke the neighbors. I wanted her to know loud and clear that I am alive and well.

This did not prove to be enough for Betsy, and she invited me again, "Show me you are real."

This time I told her, "Return to the same place, but in the afternoon of September 4th. Go up into the foothills, and I will direct you where to go as you walk, but this time come alone."

Betsy agreed, and on the afternoon of September 4th got out of her car once again and started her trek up the mountain. I told her which path to take, when to turn left and when to turn right, and then finally she arrived at a large, smooth rock just the right size for sitting down and resting. I told her, "Now you can sit and rest here and you will see me."

Betsy said distinctively, "Are you sure I can see you now?" and I assured her, "Yes, you will see me. Sit here," I spoke.

So Betsy-Morgan turned to sit on the rock and reached with her right hand to allow herself to sit gently down. As she extended her hand, she placed it upon a lizard and screamed. Immediately she heard my laughter as I said, "You think you're ready to see me, and yet you jump when you see a lizard. How much more afraid would you be if you saw me?"

She was happy with this and agreed to accept that she was speaking to a real being of light, but not prepared yet to see how I would appear to her physically.

I want to share with all of you that we are real, but we do not look like you. Our hearts are like yours. We love. We are spiritually connected to the All That Is, and we want universal peace. This is why we are here.

And until the ego subsides in the belief in separation as real, we cannot make our appearance. For we do not want to bring more fear, but alleviate it. When you are sufficiently ready, we will make our appearance, not only spiritually and energetically, but physically as well.

The final experience we feel is a highlight of the star beings moving consciously into Betsy-Morgan's awareness was in 1991 just prior to Orion's entry.

We found Betsy-Morgan needed to be cleansed out, just as you do, before she could move up in frequency to make contact with us. In order for her to be prepared, three Pleiadians were dispatched to her.

We impressed her thoughts successfully to go to see a psychologist for counseling that she thought had to do with a relationship. Yet as soon as she sat down to talk to this lovely woman, she was sufficiently relaxed where we could enter into her.

Betsy-Morgan thought she was going to be talking about her relationship, but instead, as soon as she closed her eyes, what she saw to her surprise were three elongated, blue Pleiadians, two male and one female, moving into her energy field, and going at it, as you might imagine three people frantically cleaning out an attic that was stored for 40 years with junk. The image Betsy-Morgan saw was them throwing junk, hand over fist, out of the clutter in her body/mind.

The faster they worked, the more Betsy-Morgan cried, and she said to them, "What are you doing?"

The Pleiadians responded, "You cannot do the work you have planned to do with all of this junk in you. We have got to clean out your emotional and mental field to prepare you to move ahead with the higher energies."

Betsy-Morgan literally went through an entire box of tissues. Her therapist sat there with eyes as big as saucers as Betsy-Morgan tried to explain to her what was happening. To this day, Betsy-Morgan does not know who was more surprised—her or this unsuspecting therapist.

At the end of the hour, Betsy-Morgan was emotionally exhausted, but exhilarated, feeling lighter. She was cleansed, cleansed enough for us then to make contact with her from the higher realms of light.

This is important for you to know, as all of you need to be sufficiently cleansed emotionally, physically and mentally before you can lift into the higher frequencies.

If you have a conscious intention to work with the ascension energies, to channel, to be a psychic, or a healer, you will find that you, too, will go through escalated emotional cleansing. Be aware of this, rather than afraid. Know it is part of the process, and that all is well. Feel free to find a metaphysical therapist or even a friend.

Remember, we too are your friends, although invisible ones, and when you feel like crying, we will sit with you.

Do not count your tears, but bless them. It is one of the ways you release the past and all negativity associated with it. Let it go. You will feel better after-wards, lifted, lighter and freer than ever before and more available to the higher light that will speak to you and through you when you are ready.

That was Betsy-Morgan's very first experience with the Pleiadians. Soon after that, they wrote a book through her called *A Message of Love from Your Family in the Stars, the Pleiades*. This book has yet to be published.

Allow yourself to recall, if you will, dear reader, the times in your life when you had similar experiences. Choose now to validate these experiences, and in your conscious validation, you will find yourself collecting more and greater experiences from us, your family of the stars.

The more often we connect in this way, the stronger your energy will come as well as your preparation for the ascension process that will occur in December of 2012. This moment in time will be like a portal from one level of reality to another, from one dimension called the third to a higher dimension called the fifth.

We are here with you now preparing you as best we can according to your individual willingness and readiness for this moment in time.

4
How to Prepare for Ascension

Dear ones, this will be a simple and short chapter. We know this will go against the grain of the ego, for it likes everything to be long and complex in order to believe it to be true. But this is not so. The truth is simple. Give yourself permission to believe this simplicity. You will conserve your energy for more fun activities.

Since the process of ascension is the increasing of frequency and the integration of such into your body/mind, you can best prepare for this by, first, having fun and being happy. Yes, although you may resist this, having fun and being happy increases your frequency.

Please give to yourself more time for fun activities. We laugh as we say to you, you may have to schedule fun into your life, for we know you always want, above all else, to be productive. But we want to ask you one simple question: "Are you having fun?" If you are not having fun, what is the point? Please laugh every day.

That is the best thing you can do for yourself as you prepare to ascend.

Second, be aware of your drama. The reason we say this is the ego loves a drama. It is like your soap operas. Do any of you still watch soap operas? Would it be difficult for you to stop? If you could choose to simply begin by having a sense of humor about your drama, that would lessen your hold on it.

The ego wants you to believe in the value of pain, fear, grief, jealousy, shame, blame and suffering. Does your drama have any of these? Ask yourself, "What value does having this emotion give me? Do I feel like a better person because I suffer? Do I feel I need to suffer in order to receive a reward of happiness?"

Dear beloved one, you can give up this belief right now. You cannot enter into the kingdom of heaven with these low emotions.

Find value in being happy. Give yourself permission to let life be easy. Even when you find yourself judging yourself for being too happy, laugh. Catch yourself in the act. Break your old pattern and choose to love for no other reason than you are worth it.

Thirdly, let yourself sleep more. Oh yes, we know you will resist this one for you still believe in time. Your belief in time has gotten you into a great deal of difficulty. If you have the belief you do not have enough time, you know the result you will get. The result is you will not have enough time. Do you not wish to change this belief?

Remember, the only way you can change a belief is through action. You must bust the belief by taking action that is congruent with what you want to believe is true. Going to bed earlier or sleeping later will help you to negate the useless belief in a lack of time. It will also, and this is of equal importance, help your physical body to integrate the higher frequencies.

Higher frequencies are bombarding your planet right now, and they are bombarding your physical body as well. This will result in a feeling of being tired. Please let your vehicles rest. This additional resting period will help you in integrating the higher frequencies. These frequencies are being used to help heal your body and to make physical changes in how your body looks, heals and lives.

You are actually making transmutations to the physical body while in this singular incarnation. This is the lifetime you have been dying to live. And, for your information, incarnation is a fact. Please give to yourself more rest.

Fourthly, allow yourself to take long soaks in a lovely, hot tub of water. Have wonderful reading material, and include candles, salts and fragrances if you like.

Many of you came from the sea before you incarnated finally as a human being. It will be nice for you to go back into that old environment. Allow yourself, if you want, to just sink into the warm water and close your eyes. Take a few relaxing breaths, and thank yourself for being here. Choose conscious, loving and supportive thoughts for taking time out to soak in a hot tub of water.

Tell yourself how good you are being to yourself, to the planet, and what a contribution you are making.

Feel the angels and the fairies all around you, loving you, healing you and lifting your consciousness. Remember, the simple act of kindness increases frequency and thus prepares you and others for ascension.

Fifth, sing more songs or listen to more music that uplifts you. Good music has high frequency. Frequency of this kind will move itself into your aura, cleansing your aura of all negativity and leaving you at a pristine cleansed and higher point.

Only listen or sing to music that inspires you. Much of the music that is popular today does not assist in the cleansing and healing of the auric field. Try to stay away from this "noise." It does not help you, nor does it help anyone. It promotes negativity and acts of violence. Music is meant to sooth and to heal.

Be around plants, flowers and animals. The energy and the frequency from these loving beings of light will help to heal and sooth your aura. As you send silent messages of gratitude to these loving beings, they will send loving messages of gratitude back to you that are very healing and uplifting.

Next, read good books. See good movies. Be with good people. Meditate, pray and channel. These activities help you to connect to beings of light and integrate to the higher frequencies of love.

Finally, take walks, stretch, and easily exercise your physical vehicle. This will help your body to detox and to grow into assimilating higher frequencies. Heavy exercise is not needed.

Let go of the past. Stop thinking about it. Laugh. Do more activities that make you happy.

40

———

ASCENSION

5
What Will Occur for Planet Earth

Many light beings—but not everyone on the planet Earth we would call a light being—have been noticing the changes of frequency through the escalation of time, the speedup. Things are happening faster. There is a sense of loss of time. How did so much occur in such a short period of time? This is one of the signs of the higher frequencies.

You might have found yourselves tired or irritable. You may have found yourself shaky, requiring different eating or drinking habits. Your biological clocks might have gotten turned topsy-turvy. All of this is new frequencies re-synchronizing themselves with your body/mind. It is an unlocking to a higher consciousness.

Sometimes you may feel scattered, as if you have no brain at all. And indeed you will not need your brain as you once did, for you will be using higher mind. The use of higher mind is one reason why the term intuition has become so popular in your culture. Human beings as a species will rely much more on their innate basic instincts and intuition as you move into the next few years and into the higher millennia.

You will learn how to turn on the higher mind frequencies to reach into the divine plan and not need to follow rules constructed by man that are at a lower level of vibration and used to safeguard the well being, even the life and death, of human beings.

Many of you are moving nonstop into your own demise unaware. You refuse all of the signs that have been offered that things are changing. You prefer to feel you can continue to fix things at the level of the problems in which they were created, but that time is running out.

There is a change occurring, and it has been planned for a long, long time. The reason there are so many light beings on the planet Earth is you will serve as you might imagine 'traffic cops,' helping to direct the flow of things, helping to explain to others what is occurring. This change of frequency will continue big time.

When we spoke of your brain/mind patterns changing, you will find you will need less of the structured, methodical, organizing faction of your mind as you synchronize yourself more into the channeled state or your intuited faculties. When these take over, your thoughts as well as your actions will be influenced by the divine, and all of you will be orchestrated in harmony like a synchronized dance working towards the common good of the whole.

In these future times of which we speak, there will be no competition. That is hard for the brain of a human being to even begin to understand at this time, for your culture is so based on getting ahead. It takes a while to bring in this new idea and allow it to integrate, to take hold, because it goes against everything the human race has been taught.

Let it be made plain and simple: There is change upon you and this change is good. At first it will feel disturbing, because it is unfamiliar. But let us repeat, this change is good. You are moving from one frequency to another higher frequency, and this one, simple statement makes all the difference. It will make a huge difference.

Can you imagine a world in which there is no competition? Can you imagine a world in which no one is striving to get ahead? Where everyone wants to live in harmony and actually sees more value in oneness than in separation? Can you imagine a world where everyone is willing to trust God, to listen to their own imagination and call it higher truth and wisdom?

Can you imagine a world where human beings are willing to give up control? We are not saying that you need to give up free will. This is entirely different. You will still have volition to choose love or fear, but the flow of who you are will be flowing in the direction of harmony.

There will be a desire or impulse within you, a silent value of union and cooperation that will influence everything you do, and this is all due to the shift in frequency.

In this new world, for indeed mark our words it will be a new world, there will be a higher order of things. By this time, the governments and the controlling factions of the world will have changed. You will not have the governments you have today, with all the need for so many global rules, wars and enforcement. The people will be willing and wanting to live in harmony.

This world of safety will allow each one of you to have more energy for your creative outlets. Over time, the frontal lobe of your brain will increase, and you will notice your foreheads getting larger. This will be due to your creative and intuitive faculties finally being allowed to emerge.

Your children will be born with many of their spiritual gifts intact. Some, the rainbow children, will even remember their past lives, and others will remember what life was like beyond the veil or before they reincarnated. Everyone will accept reincarnation as fact. There will be no need to review books that say anything to the contrary, for there will be a great understanding from love of why these contradictory books were even written.

Forgiveness will be so natural that it will even bypass the act of blame. All will be understood.

Many souls that come in will be able to do spontaneous healing of the body or the emotions for others who are severely or chronically ill. For some, it will just require being in their presence. You may have noticed some of this has already begun in degrees. This will grow in expression, grow in physicality greatly.

Basically what is happening to your planet is you are moving into enlightenment. Enlightenment, too, comes in degrees, but you can only expand just so quickly without desecrating yourselves. Your bodies could not stand that much heat.

It is excellent many of you have now taken to different forms of dematerializing the body, such as channeling, meditation, yoga, chanting and healing. These are all access tools to a higher reality, a reality that is connecting to your pineal and stimulating new functions of your glandular system as it increases and stimulates awakening or higher awareness.

You are connected to a pole of light that is extending itself into your planet now and aligns itself with the pole that goes through your planet, through from the North Pole to the South Pole and is beginning to vibrate at a higher frequency. This vibration will get stronger and stronger, and those who are attuned to it now will open even more.

Side-effects could include headaches as well as various body aches and pains and nausea.

As the vibration increases, it will also affect weather patterns and physical disruptions on your planet Earth. Your Earth will not be destroyed, but will go through great changes as well.

We now want to tell you something that is shocking and may be difficult to comprehend, but it is truth of the highest level. Allow yourselves to go there, beyond the physical meaning of the words. You are moving closer to a state of causal being.

When this happens, in the very moment it happens, there will come a splitting apart and a great amount of energy will be released. It will be the sudden release of the old, smaller self and the moving into the higher, awakened self.

Much of your memory patterns associated with the ego and your past will be lost and forgotten, and simultaneously that part that cares about remembering it will not care but feel greatly calm, exhilarated and free, ready to focus on the present moment, realizing that love can only be found here and now.

The residue of gratitude from any past, loving experiences will remain in your heart chakra, and the more gratitude different human beings felt, the more there will be an aura of pink emanating from that chakra.

Those who have the most pink will generally be the better healers. And to those people, we say, "Do indeed protect yourself and have good boundaries."

Human beings will begin to see the spectra of colors coming from the auras and will know the gifts you bring according to your colors.

Some human beings will wish to gravitate to you because of your wonderful healing energy. To you we say, "Allow yourselves to rest and have fun and have good boundaries."

We pause for a moment to reference the fact that even though you will have grown into a fifth-dimensional state, there will be degrees of awareness in the fifth-dimensional state. Some of you who have made this transition will be highly aware while others less aware. The good news is, it will be so much easier to be compassionate and helpful to those who are less aware.

We take special joy in sharing with you that the babies who are to come will be remarkable for your planet. They will bring much knowledge and information from their different and various stars. When this happens, the children will teach the adults, and the adults will listen, for they will recognize that the wisdom is still intact.

And then we, your family from the stars, can return, for you will not be so afraid of us. There will be books written by the children. They will speak the truth, while the adults who can will write from their words.

There will be new music, new frequencies, new ideas, new options that all come in with the children. There will be more respect of children.

We find sharing with you the changes that are about to come unto your planet very exciting, for we know many of you will be motivated to talk about these changes with the same excitement we bring to you now … and this is good, because these changes are not meant to make anyone afraid, but to create an opening or an allowance of ease and trust, knowing the changes are good.

As the mass consciousness prepares in this way through trust, willingness and ease, you will begin to have more sightings of spacecraft. We will continue to remain respectful to your emotional level of awareness and not frighten you. When the mass consciousness is ready, we will make our entrance once again and form not just a global community but a galactic community.

Orion has been instrumental as what you might call a Commander-in-Chief to oversee this restructuring. We in the Galactic Command Fleet are very grateful to Orion for his work and assistance. He will continue to assist individually as well as globally until all are set in place.

Those beings who prepare for this change by doing activities to increase and strengthen their frequency will make the shift into higher consciousness more easily.

Let us explain: We will use the example of a vehicle, such as your automobiles driving down a freeway. Let us say a smaller automobile that is not in good shape driving at a slower speed runs into a cardboard box. This cardboard box represents resistance, a negative experience. The vehicle will experience a larger impact, a stronger sound and perhaps more of the frequency of the reaction of fear.

On the other hand, a larger vehicle, more powerful, moving at a faster speed or frequency, moving down the same highway could hit the same cardboard box and not even know it was there, not even hear a sound or feel an impact.

We are attempting to give to you an example of how you can be prepared. Everything is relative according to your perceptions, and when you are vibrating at a higher frequency, fear is not one of your options.

It is more of learning to hold your focus on love until holding your focus on love becomes automatic and there is no effort at all. It just is, and then all the objects that are in opposition to love are inconsequential, as if they are simply not at all. Life becomes easier and happier for everyone.

So, this is where you all are moving. This is an invitation to go to the fifth dimension now. Everyone will get there eventually, but not everyone will get there now. 'Now' means the time between this present moment and the end of 2012.

At the beginning of 2013 will come an opportunity to integrate this new energy. Everything is building towards this moment. Everything you do between now and December of 2012 will count in your favor of preparing to move into Heaven on Earth. This is called ascension.

As we have said before in other writings, some people will move to the left and some will move to the right in that moment. You will not necessarily know who moves to the left or who moves to the right. In that level of awareness, those who have chosen the higher frequency of love and harmony will simply experience love and harmony, while those who are still captivated and believing in fear and drama will continue to experience more fear and drama. And this is where free will enters.

What you can do to best prepare yourselves for this shift called ascension is to become more consciously aware of choosing thoughts and responses coming from love. The more often you do this, the more emotionally balanced and in harmony you will be with the higher plan and more in alignment with your own higher self.

You will automatically feel and essentially be expanded. You will begin to harness some of the available universal power and open your chakras to higher light, which will begin automatically moving you into your light body. When this happens, it is like having a spiritual coat of armor. Negativity cannot affect you like it did when you were 'simply human.' You will have moved into higher consciousness.

6
Exercices

This is the time of times, a time some have referred to as the Apocalypse, a time some have referred to as the Second Coming. We would like to say it is a re-birth, the reemergence of the Christ consciousness on Earth.

The Mayan culture was correct in its assessment that this is drawing to the end of times, but it is the end of third-dimensional times for those who are choosing to live in higher awareness.

Dear Earth beings, remember that you can prepare yourself for ascension. You prepare yourself through love. If there was ever a time to be willing to give and receive love, it is now.

Remember the words to the song *Nature Boy*: "The greatest thing that ever was is just to love and be loved in return." Let this be your mantra for the next three and a half years, and just let everything else go.

Believe us when we say conflict is not important. You are learning how to literally rise in love. Love is a frequency, and as you do, feel, say and act in all things loving, you will be lifting into the fifth dimension. You will be going home.

This action is the precursor of all that is to be, and it is remembered through your actions that you pave the way to your successfully achieving harmony and integration in this higher frequency.

There will be the presence of saints and angels when you arrive, and upon that day, this statement will be more easily understood and assimilated. We know when you read it here now, it may just feel like a figment of your imagination. Yet between now and then, you will come to see how very important your imagination really is in the manifestation of things.

So let us give to you now an exercise for cleansing the old and exercise for manifesting the new.

***

Exercise for Cleansing

Dear beloveds, this exercise for cleansing will include the cleansing of your emotional, mental and physical bodies. Upon completion of this, you will notice basically two things: Easier manifestation of that which you wish to have in your life, but a bit of a rocky road while you complete the releasing of old patterns.

Please remember to be patient with yourself. Please remember, you do not do these exercises alone. Learn to call upon your angels of light. We are always here to help you and can do more if you call upon us. You may be specific in your requests, asking for an angel to help cleanse, another to help protect, and another to help manifest. We are so happy when you call upon us.

We want you to know that each one of you has your own ascension angel. An ascension angel is an archangel. Some of you will have the same archangel.

We want you to know we can work with many of you at one time. That is no problem to us. We share a group consciousness field, and when one person ascends or moves forward, it helps the entire group.

The exercise of light used for cleansing is this: Allow yourself to sit in a comfortable and relaxed position. Close your eyes and take a nice, deep, relaxing breath. Drop into your heart and ask for the presence of Orion, your ascension angel and your cleansing angel.

You may begin to see us. Trust this. You may even receive a name. Trust this.

You may speak the name out loud. If the name is accurate, it will feel good to you. If it is not accurate, continue to allow the name to redefine itself until you feel it is a fit. The names are not as important to us as they are to you.

At this time, take another deep, relaxing breath. Allow yourself to imagine a beautiful white light pouring into the top of your aura, moving down through your chakra system and filling your entire auric field with beautiful white light. Imagine this white light moving through every chakra.

Let the white light move through the base chakra until you see all the light leaving as a pure red. Say to yourself, *I now cleanse, heal and balance my first chakra.*

Allow the light to pour through your head to chakra two and see the light leaving here a beautiful, pure orange. Again say to yourself, *I allow myself to be cleansed, healed and balanced.*

Breathe in the white light and go to chakra three. See the light leave here as yellow. Repeat your cleansing instructions.

Continue to chakra four and see the light leave a pure green, and then to your throat a beautiful blue, your third eye a beautiful purple, and your crown a beautiful white.

Feel the radiance, feel the harmony, feel the peace. Let more white light pour in and rinse through every cell and every chakra, and one last time say to yourself, *I am cleansed, I am healed and I am balanced.*

Now ask for the sword of Archangel Michael to cut the cords of any negative person, place or thing, and think to yourself, *Only love remains. I release these people and circumstances to the light. May they be loved and blessed and healed according to their willingness to receive love.*

Ask for yourself, *I am loved, blessed, healed, cleansed and protected now.*

Allow a beautiful, golden cocoon of light to be placed all around you. Imagine it ten feet thick. See all the colors of your chakras emanating fully, strong, whole, complete. Feel a surge of physical vitality, a sense of well being, connection to God, inner peace, prosperity of every good thing, self love.

Think to yourself, *I deserve this goodness. I am one with the light. I am a child of light, and I allow myself to inherit the kingdom of Heaven now.*

As my cup runneth over, I allow this light to spill forth, nourishing all who would receive this love. I am cleansed and protected. And so it is.

Thanking your angels and guides who helped you, allow yourself to become grounded by wiggling your fingers and toes and coming back into your body. When you feel sufficiently grounded, you may continue your day.

Allow yourself to do this exercise as many times a day as you feel you need it. Since you are moving more into your light body, you may find yourself more susceptible to negative energies, but with a quick review of this exercise, you will soon be able to easily remove them. Trust your own power and ours. God wants you to be happy, healthy and experience your own truth.

***

Exercise for Manifestation

Next is an exercise for manifestation. Allow yourself to sit in a comfortable and relaxed position. Close your eyes and know that this exercise is most important when you are feeling insecure or uncertain about your financial prosperity and well being.

Ask for a pure, white light to come over you to rinse through every cell of your being. As the light pours out and radiates forth from you, feel and see the light turn to a beautiful pink. This is the pink light of love.

Allow yourself to feel love and reverence for who you are. Feel this pink light expand around your heart. Feel your heart grow until this pink light encompasses your entire body.

Notice there is a pink light of love coming from the universe as well, and this pink light quickly en-velopes you.

Feel how large you feel and how you are one with the whole of All That Is. Allow yourself to think, *I am embraced by love.*

I forgive myself. I forgive myself of all thoughts that were harmful to me or to anyone else. I forgive anyone else of any thought or action that was hurtful towards me or another person. I release the past. I am grateful for the lessons the past has given to me, and I accept now that only love remains. I accept that this love harmonizes in my heart, my body, my emotions, my thoughts and my life now.

I am in harmony with the universe and with the greater good. I release resistance to love, and I allow God to give to me the fullness of his love. I give thanks for this love, which comes to me in all forms. I allow love in the form of wonderful relationships, perfect health, peace of mind, and financial prosperity.

Now take a moment to feel this energy flowing into your body. Literally breathe it in. See dollar bills that say $100, $1,000. Feel them coming into your body. Feel what you would do with that money, that you would give it to others, and there would be more than you could ever give away. Feel yourself spending money to assist the economy.

Feel yourself spending money on yourself and how good that feels. No shame, no blame. Feel yourself contributing to charitable organizations or starting one of your own ... and still there is money, more than you can possibly spend. Let yourself feel how good that is.

This is the truth. We live in a prosperous universe. It is time for you to make a withdrawal. The more you withdraw, the more you have. This is the truth. Not the reverse, because it is like love.

The more you give, the more you have to give. The more you let God love you, the more God *can* love you. Learn to live by truth and not by fable, and through your own experience you will see love everywhere.

The key here is to recognize you have so much that you can share it infinitely and abundantly. If you try to hold onto the money that starts to flow into your life, it will slow down the flow. Remember it is a flow.

The moment you start to hoard it, please recognize there is a subconscious thought of lack. Allow the flow and it will get stronger and stronger like a river running to its source.

You cannot hold love back from itself once recognized as truth. Just continue to feel how good it feels to have all of this wealth running through you.

If you have any thought to the contrary, let it be rinsed away by love itself and returned to the wonderful feeling of infinite wealth and prosperity.

Think to yourself, *I am a creator of good. Everywhere I go I bring a frequency of wealth. This frequency I carry helps to heal everyone's consciousness, therefore I am a benefactor.*

I love this. I love myself. I love the wealth of the universe. The universe and I are one. I accept I am a window to the soul of God, and I let wealth flow through me in ever increasing measure now and always.

Feeling this wonderful goodness as you go about your day. Do this exercise as often as you wish.

If you place your fingers at your temples and tap your temples three times, and think to yourself, *I am infinitely wealthy, I am a millionaire, I have more money than I could possibly spend, and I love spending my money and sharing my money; I have more money than I could possibly spend; I spend and share my money infinitely with everyone*, what will happen is that this will feed your subconscious mind with the thoughts of truth, and you will begin to harmonize with your universal good. You will soon see you cannot keep it from you.

The first thoughts of the ego will be to stop it, for you will feel guilty. This is the old thought of the third dimension. When this occurs, simply notice it. Have a sense of humor about it, and with a few deep breaths, breathe the old away. Cut the cords, and only love remains.

Breathe in new life, harmony and prosperity, over and over again, loving yourself more and more with every breath, until eventually you will feel very good and happy and grateful with being infinitely wealthy.

Just think of how much good you can do as one of God's emissaries of wealth upon the planet Earth. Thank you for your contribution. We appreciate it, and so will you.

***

Exercise for De-stressing

Beloveds, there are moments throughout your day when each one of you feels a bit stressed. Stress is due to believing in a false thought. Whenever you are stressed, it is a signal to yourself to remind you that you can choose again. You are creating your own reality by the thoughts you choose to believe are real.

Whenever you are stressed, sit in a comfortable and relaxed position and ask for an angel of ease to come to you, an angel of calm, and an angel of truth. Ask to harmonize with universal truth. Breathe deeply into the divine mind and feel that mind flowing into your aura, sweeping clean all false thoughts. Think to yourself, *I will have no false idol.* A false idol is a false thought. You remember that it is God's pleasure to love you, for you to be happy.

Have you ever seen a child playing, free of worry? That is how God wants you to be. If you truly want to serve God, think of that image, place yourself into that image, and let yourself be the child. As you sit in this relaxed way, see the child playing carefree. Become the child, and play in your heart, and as you imagine playing, all those other thoughts will leave you.

The mind will attempt to grab them and make them real. Keep focusing on being carefree and playing. Let us replace the thoughts with thoughts of love, joy and harmony.

You do not need to strive in the world of form, because when your consciousness is healed, everything will come to you naturally, easily when you need and want it. It is through your belief that you must do things in the physical world that creates the need to do things in the physical world. It is the belief that you must work hard for a living that creates the reality of working hard for a living.

In order to change this reality, begin with the power of your wonderful imagination. Imagine the reality you love, and feel it to be true. That frequency transmutes the harsh world of the third dimension. It erases it, because higher frequency always wins. The more often you imagine and feel what it is you want, the more easily you will move into a higher reality of truth.

Just keep repeating this exercise as often as you wish. Feel carefree and at ease, and everything that was worrying you will fall away. You will see.

Remember, you cannot heal the problem at the level at which it was created. Everything is yours through right of consciousness. Learn to work from the inner and not the outer. This is the way of the new tomorrow, and you are preparing for the new tomorrow by practicing these exercises of light today.

***

Exercise for Ascension
(the Heart of this Book)

Our beloved beings of light, the process of ascension is the lifting of frequency. When frequency lifts, consciousness is healed. When consciousness is healed, you perceive your reality to be a happier, healthier, more loving and joyful experience.

Therefore, if you would like this result, allow yourself to participate in ascension freely at least once a day. It only takes three to fifteen minutes to fully enjoy this exercise of light.

To begin, sit in a comfortable and relaxed position and close your eyes. Take several relaxing breaths and drop into your heart. Here in your heart invite me, Orion, to assist you.

I am a being of light who oversees ascension. I am here to help all Earth beings who would like to increase their frequency and to move into the fifth dimension.

As you call upon me, you may begin to feel light-headed, lifted, easy, calm and blissful. You may even feel swirls of energy, for my energy comes to you in spirals.

Sitting in this comfortable and relaxed position, breathing easily with your eyes closed, invite the Orion energies to help you to ascend. I will move in, in a counterclockwise motion, around and around. As you sit, you may feel this.

My first process will be to remove or nullify negative thinking and imbalanced emotions. I will literally swirl them out of your auric field, cleansing your aura, your body and the room in which you sit. As this process happens, you automatically lift. This is because you are light.

This that was taken from you were simply untruths or illusions made real through your belief in them or through your assigning value to them. When you choose love and light instead, this gives me the permission I need to help you. I will never come uninvited. I will respect your free will.

Continuing to sit in this way, take high thoughts of love such as: *I am willing to lift into my light body. I wish to live the path of my soul. I live in integrity with my higher self. I align with God's plan. Thy will be done.*

Remembering God's will is always for your happiness: *I am willing to lift into love and light. I allow myself to easily and lovingly move into the fifth dimension.*

I open to my spiritual gifts. I feel my passion for life, and I feel the courage to live life fully. I care again, because I know I can make choices that support my well being.

I give thanks, and I lift higher and higher. I invite my angels of light and my ascension angels to come close and help me now. I align with the highest light possible. I allow this light to harmonize and integrate in me now, and I bring in my highest truth.

I am that I am. I am one with God now, and I am at peace.

Allow yourself to sit and to hold this feeling and this frequency for a few moments. One to three minutes is enough, but feel comfortable if you would like to relax in this for fifteen minutes. Just breathe, relax and surrender to high and loving thoughts.

As you sit in this way, you may begin to feel, hear and see in the higher realms. The higher realms will be exposed to you as you rise in frequency.

You may even meet your spirit guides and angels. You may always ask us, "Do you come in love?" We always tell you the truth. And if you want us to leave, just ask us to. We are here to help you, not to make you afraid. You may ask us to work with you for special reasons, and we will do our best. We will let you know if we cannot do certain tasks, but we love to hear what you would like us to do.

As you continue to rise higher, continue to relax and simply be open to whatever occurs on the higher realms. Integrating this frequency deeply, and releasing negativity of all forms, embrace the light.

Integrate this light into every cell, and then, when you are ready, slowly, gently, easily and completely come back into your body now. You may wiggle your fingers and toes, squeeze your knees and get grounded before you move about your day.

Each time you do this ascension exercise, you will align more with your body of light and less with the physical. This will result in the ego dying. Since the ego does not want to die, it will attempt to get your attention through various means such as feelings of guilt, fear or anger. Just be on the lookout for this, and have a sense of humor.

Remember to choose laughter, love and acts of kindness for yourself and others. Give yourself ample rest, water, and fun activities. Keep trusting the process, breathe, invite us to help you. All will be well.

You are moving through the preparation for ascension. With your courage and willingness to continue, you will soon be on the other side and your goal, Heaven on Earth, is assured.

Thank you for your valiant efforts. You will be rewarded by the love you have always been looking for.

7
Angels Among You

Be willing to look out for your children. Angels are coming in now to help you. The children who are coming in are going to have amazing gifts and strength of character.

You will know us. We will almost glow. We are here to help make your ascension easier and more possible. We are here to teach you wonderful things.

The gift to be as a child is not always as simple as it looks, but it is, above all else, a necessary gift. Those of you who have children around, consider yourself blessed, for they are there to help you to remember what is important. Do not let the third-dimensional world get the best of you. If it does, you are believing in it too much.

Remember, it is only a school room. You constructed it so you could learn, and what you are learning is love. As soon as you truly learn love, that school room will disappear.

Play with the children more. Play as a child when you are not around them. Love being childlike. Be carefree.

You can be a lily in the field. This is your time to remember who you are. Look to the children.

There will be angels among you, and we always, always love and forgive you, even if you forget. Bless yourselves daily, feel grateful and forgiving, and know above all else you are always loved.

Thank you for reading this message. We will keep the vibration clear all around you, and all you need to do is ask for the energy of ascension. It is as simple as that. Let it be.

Part II

THE GIFT OF THE SHIFT

68

———

ASCENSION

8
Focus and Frequency

Indeed, beloved beings of light, this is a combination of Hatshepsut and Orion. Indeed, there are the angels all around us, encircling us as lace does with a doily. But the main frequency, indeed, comes from Hatshepsut and Orion, for we wish to bring to you a very strong frequency of love. For we in this time tell you that you are warrior angels on a planet needing your assistance.

We would like to talk briefly about the shift. We would like to tell you what we feel will be a cornerstone for you and how you can prepare for what is occurring. Generally speaking, the shift most holy is about change. This change can be perceived, as all things can be perceived, either with fear or love. To the degree you are already choosing to perceive whatever happens in your life lovingly, you will perceive the shift in the same manner.

The only spiritual learning you can really take with you is what you practice when you are unconsciously responding to life. We would now bring up a word, a word you don't necessarily like—discipline. Discipline. The word 'disciple' comes from it, and what would a disciple be but a follower of a belief.

We know that all of your beliefs define you and perhaps limit you, but some are good beliefs and point you in the right direction, such as the belief that you are a child of light, the belief that you are eternal, the belief that you are one with God, the belief that you are infinitely more powerful than circumstance, for you are that which attracted it. All of these beliefs begin the process of freedom.

As you allow yourself to modify beliefs, to change them, and to adopt helping, healing, holy beliefs, you begin to demonstrate in your life more personal freedom and power, and therefore more joy in all you do.

But this is not necessarily an easy path, because what we are speaking of goes to the level of the conscious and the subconscious mind. Your subconscious mind is a level of creativity.

So, you must practice a belief, think about a belief, focus on a belief, over and over and over, until it moves into your unconscious level of being, where you automatically respond from it without thought.

Sometimes we hear you saying, "But I …," "But I …," "But I …." We want you to know that if a belief is in your subconscious, you will attract its outcome. That's a law.

So right now we say to you what is coming is change and how you choose to perceive it will come from what you have practiced.

We say to you it is true that like attracts like, and so we bring up the word 'frequency.' What is your frequency? It is like a thermostat, you know. Do you keep it on 60? 70? 75? Surely not 80. A bit uncomfortable at 80.

You may want to consider readjusting your spiritual thermostat. And how in the world can you do that? Oh beloved beings of light, it is not too late. You have arrived on the scene at the right time and the right day and the right channel, for we say to you truly that frequency comes from feeling, and feeling comes from choice of thought.

Do you know that your thought is the most powerful thing, the most powerful force that you have available to you on your Earth plane?

It is like water creating the canyon, the great canyon, and your thought can begin to change your life, because it is the precursor to an emotion, and an emotion is a vibration.

So, dear ones, we begin Part II with (1) there is a shift, (2) the shift means change, change upon the planet, which is the physical, and change in the inner, which is the consciousness of all mankind.

The change will occur for you in duplicates: One, coming from your frequency, your free will, your power of choice, your thought, and two, it will come to you with *how* you and *who* you choose to identify with in mass consciousness.

Who do you identify with? Well, human beings, of course. What are some of the other identities? For you, we feel you are in a very good group. You are in a group that is beginning to recognize that you have power, and this power is not to manipulate, but it is shared love. That as you love another, you love yourself, and as you love yourself, you are free to love another.

So, you are growing in great harmony with your group mass consciousness. What you are attracting to you, you are attracting through you.

Now this has been set in motion a long time ago by you and by others who are ancient of days. Much has been written about the Mayan calendar, and there is going to be a great change on your planet Earth. There will be many shakeups, and you can see them happening now. You can see the devastation on your planet, and it will continue. Practically every week now, you will hear of something.

Yes, it is very good to send energy. It is very good to send prayer. It is better to send positive visualization than it is to worry and forget to pray. Why? Because, dear ones, we tell you most importantly that which we have come to speak with you about. You are, at one level and at one level only, a human being. You appear to be flesh and solid, but who you are is not contained by the barrier of your skin. Let us talk about that for just a moment.

You have a human body. This human body has frequency. It is the most dense frequency of a representation of who you are. But you also have what you call an aura. Let us talk about this.

You have your human body and extending from that you have, let us say, the first level of your aura, which would be your emotional body. Then at a dif-ferent frequency you have your mental body, then extended out from that you have a spiritual body, and extended out from that you have an astral field.

Now, you do not travel in that astral field unless you are asleep at night and connected by that which you know as a silver cord. But you are very aware of your auras one, two and three—the emotional body, the mental body, and the spiritual body.

Those of you who are very emotionally inclined spend a lot of time in your emotional body, and many people will be able to see the colors of your aura. And those of you who are sharp, mentally speaking, we would say you spend more time in the mental body, and you would make a good seer or psychic. Those in the emotional body will feel and intuit and have instinct. Now this third body has a very, very high frequency. It is your spiritual body.

All of you have been, in many lifetimes, striving for enlightenment. You will have moments of vibrating at this frequency, moments of feeling this level of spiritual connection with the All That Is. Sometimes when you channel, you will actually expand your awareness of who you are and feel the lightening up through all of the levels of who you are—body, mind, emotions and spirit. You will feel so light and free.

It is not beneficial for you to move into the astral plane, for when you do so, you would just not want to come back. So, you are tethered, let us say, to this subtle energy body that makes up your identity.

In your bodies, in your aura and your physical body, you have, let us say, a library of knowledge, and we might say it is contained in your DNA and in the frequency bodies that are vibrating all around you. When you are operational, and you always are, your energy field will pick up impressions from other people and other places.

Some of you are very geographically connected, let us say, and when there is a disturbance on your Earth plane, you may feel emotionally upset. This is because you are physically, truly in reality, connected to all that is. You are connected to every person, every place, and everything through the subtle energy body of your aura. This is good and this is bad.

It can be seen through love, and it can be perceived through fear. So, let us take a look at that.

The love is: If you choose to keep yourself cleansed, and if you love yourself by being good to you, if you take care of your subtle energy bodies, you will grow in great harmony in self-love and in your spiritual knowledge, and you will ascend peacefully and easily into the higher dimensions. For you will gradually, in your own time, shift your identity from the physical to a lighter body.

This does not necessarily mean you will lose your physical body. It means you are bringing more light and a higher frequency to it.

But, dear ones, you need to take care of who you are at the vibrational level. We know you have become more aware of what you eat, and we know you have become more aware of exercise. We want to encourage you to become even more aware of rest and play, and these are two words we would wish to underscore this evening. Please take care of yourselves with enough rest and play.

It is time to balance your subtle energy field, because if you do not, it will weaken, and this means to you in practical terms that you will get a tear in your energy field, and you will leak energy.

Have any of you felt tired, frustrated, confused, depressed? All of you, we say. Well, let us reconsider what you might do. It is time for you to choose to practice to the point it becomes unconscious knowledge that you are a child of light. You have more than a physical body, and you have more than a physical reality. If you talk to us in channeling, does that not lend itself to the truth that you do know you have more than a physical reality?

The reality of the physical defined by the five senses has now extended for you into the higher realms, and although you cannot hear us with your physical ear, you begin to feel us with your heart and hear us with mind impressions or see us with the inner visual instincts of your inner eye. You are growing, you see, into the recognition of the higher frequencies.

If any of you channel, you are not living entirely in your physical body. And it would be very good for you, when you wake up in the morning, to call your energy back to be physical, and perhaps even think *feet*.

You have wonderful grounding chakras in your feet, and when you stand up, send your energy into the ground. Stand on Mother Earth every day, and allow yourself to reconnect with the physical.

It is difficult for you to operate in the third dimension if you are not grounded in your body, especially while you are very aware that you are consciously shifting into the higher dimensions.

As you shift in the higher dimensions, you will be spending more time in your auric field and your higher chakras. The chakra system is that which connects your physical body to your auric body. So you will want to keep your chakras clean and spinning, and you will want to keep your auric field clean and healed. How you do this, beloveds, is to allow yourself to be happy.

Do not take the thought that your being happy is someone else's responsibility. Sometimes we look at you in relationship and we see that the relationship you are in does not make you happy, and yet you continue to say, "If they would only change, I could be happy." Or, "If they would just break up with me and leave, I could be happy." We would say to you to consider not making your happiness dependent upon another person's choices, and to know you are very powerful, that you are the light I Am.

We remind you, when asked, "Who are you?" it was spoken, "I Am that I Am." You are divine. And every thought you think, every single one, is creative.

Now, here's the kicker. To the degree you are vibrating at a higher frequency, your thoughts manifest into form more quickly. And this is why we say, "focus and frequency."

It is time you consciously identify your thoughts and your feelings with joy, because in the moments when you feel you are in crisis, you could be your own betrayer or your own hero, or she-ro, depending upon where you swing when you are unconscious.

The world and the energy are shifting, and how you shift with it, with love or fear, is up to you. That which is being created around you is created from you, from your frequency and from your focus. So every day, put into practice thoughts of joy.

We would suggest you do exercises of great freedom to allow yourself, instead of thinking, "Oh dear, I'm about to become extinct," to think, "Oh my, I'm about to become bigger and lighter and freer and happier and healthier." What choice would you make if you were going to live in a planet of complete freedom and joy? What would your life look like? How good could you feel?

What is going on is for the purpose of cleansing. Do you remember that *A Course in Miracles* said, "We can allow you to mis-create only so long, and then we will intervene"? This is *intervention*. You have heard about those who are in recovery; the Earth is in recovery. We have come as intervention, and there are many, many of us. It is time to love you.

Some people may call this tough love, but it is love just the same. We are here to remind you that you still have the power, and so the words "focus and frequency" are the keys to your freedom and your movement into the Kingdom of Heaven on Earth. What would you like? It is still your choice.

So let us say to you, as you continue to notice you are not just a body, then you are the light I Am of the divine, and this body includes an auric field of emotions, of thoughts, and of the Kingdom of Heaven, your spiritual body, which you as the caretaker, as the shepherd of yourself, you can now choose daily to take care of. Now many of you may feel it is a lot of effort, but we want you to know the reward will be tenfold.

For instance, let us say, suppose you dressed a little child to go to a swim meet, and you had to get on her uniform, and you had to get all of her equipment, and you had to spray on her suntan lotion, you had to drive her across town, you had to register, you had to pay, and then she went swimming for 30 minutes, and she was out again in your arms, and you wrapped her in a towel, and you may have thought, *Was this all there was to a swim meet? I spent more time than this getting her ready.* We want you to know that your efforts are accumulative.

It requires that you begin to practice what you want to receive. And this means that every day you sit, in your own beautiful way, and feel God. Feel who you are. Feel joy, remembering it is the frequency that will manifest in your life when you are unconsciously responding to activities happening around you. How do you automatically respond?

So, dear ones, we wish to lift and cleanse and heal your energy field, so allow yourselves now to consider this be an exercise of light that you may wish to use from this day forward.

Allow yourselves then, beloved beings, to sit ye in a comfortable and relaxed position, and close your eyes. Allow yourself to drop into your heart, and take a nice, deep, relaxing breath.

And here in your heart, allow yourself to imagine, if you will, a small and beautiful pyramid of light. Allow this pyramid to begin to grow until it fills up the entire cavity of your heart and your chest, and it continues to grow. As this pyramid grows, we wish for you to feel healing love.

Allow yourself now to notice you are actually *inside* this pyramid as it continues to grow, and it gets bigger and bigger. Take a nice, deep, relaxing breath and feel how good this pyramid feels for you, and you are totally inside it now. Let it be as big as you want it to be, and first see this pyramid as golden energy, and see yourself sitting inside this pyramid very, very comfortably, and feel this golden light move all the way into your body and to begin to move through every layer of your aura.

We want you to know this golden light is now going to begin to stimulate and to activate the sleeping parts of your auric body. We now wish to activate the sleeping DNA. This golden light now moves into every layer of your aura and every cell of your body, and this golden light moves into every chakra: one, two, three, four, five, six, and seven.

And now within you is found a treasure, a little box that has a lock on it. Allow yourself to look at this treasure, this locked box. This is a secret within your DNA.

Beloveds, you have held a secret within you. You are a living library. You have moved through what is called the shift, or ascension, other times. This is your third time through, and this time you will make it.

Allow yourself to hold out your hand to receive a key, and allow yourself to see Orion, Archangel Michael, Hatshepsut, Maitreya or your personal guide coming towards you right now. Feel the energy and the power.

The key to this box is now placed in your hands. Allow yourself to look at this key and look at the treasure. How big is that lock? Would you like to open it now?

Would you like to activate the sleeping DNA that can move you towards your spiritual freedom, that can start the higher vibrations in every cell of your body and in every area of your life?

See your guides around you, and feel their unconditional love and encouragement, and if you choose, allow yourself to move towards that beautiful box, that treasure box, and place the key into the lock and open it now.

Open it wide up, and let the secret spill forth, releasing its frequency, perhaps its sound, its light, its message into your aura, into your knowledge, into your body right now. And to yourself, know, hear, see and feel what this treasure that you have been keeping locked up for hundreds of lifetimes is telling you.

And now, holding the hand of your guides and angels, allow yourself to feel and to think, *I activate my DNA now. It is my choice. I ask in the higher energies of higher love.*

Think to yourself, *I activate the DNA now. I lift into my spiritual freedom now. I am empowered, and I am one with light.*

Feel yourself fill up with golden light, and feel yourself grow and move into this pyramid, growing bigger.

And now we send to you the ancient of days and ascended masters. We send to you Hatshepsut, who hands to you a scroll. Orion and Archangel Michael and Saint Germain call to you now, the ones you would have with you, and hold out your hands to receive their gifts, and bring these gifts into you that they might vibrate with you and awaken you now.

Notice from the center of your heart another pyramid is growing and grows very quickly and very easily up through and beyond the golden pyramid, and this pyramid is green, and this is the holy pyramid.

You were here once upon a time when you received great secrets of light, and it does not require that you go back there physically. Remember, you are not just a physical body. Every thought you think communicates around the world. Every feeling you have communicates. You are energy, and you are light, and what is happening to you now is that you will not need your body in order to speak or to love, to know, to be, to go, to have or to manifest. You have a body, but you are not limited to a body.

Allow this beautiful healing energy of the green pyramid now. Notice there is a light coming from the apex, which is above your head. A pure, white light drops through the golden pyramid into the top of your head, and moves down through every chakra of your body. This is healing light and cleansing light.

Dear ones, as you open now in the coming days, we want you to be very, very aware that everything is energy; and as you open, you must remember to cleanse yourself, and when you are ready, close the doors to your auric field and the doors to your chakras.

Many human beings will not know what they are doing, and they will be releasing toxicities.

So we cleanse you out now, bring in the white light. You may feel very high and uplifted. This is coming from a very, very high source, down through the highest chakras, down through your higher self and your soul self, down through your crown, your third eye, your throat, into your heart. And allow this beautiful white light to move into every cell and release all negativity.

And now, with the sword of Archangel Michael, we cut the cord to all persons, all places, and all things that are beneath your high frequency, that are beneath your highest good. We release you to your highest good now, according to your free will to do so. If you simply agree, just think *Amen*, and notice you lift.

We cut the cord to any person, place or thing that is lower than this frequency, and assist you in simply moving away from them easily, with love and humor and healing.

Now we cleanse, cleanse, cleanse again. Breathe in. There is emotion leaving. This is good. Another deep breath.

Imagine a column of white light all the way through you. Now feel this light moving out through your body, filling up the golden pyramid, filling up the green pyramid, and everything is white light now.

Cleansing all of your chakras and all layers of your auric field, release everything but love, and allow your-self to think to yourself, *I am light. I am pure, I am whole, and I am cleansed, and I do this according to my highest good. At this time, I ask for the edges of my auric field to have a crystal protection around me so no adverse energies can come in.*

I walk in harmony and peace. I forgive and release all others, and I have good boundaries. I know from my innate intuition where I should go, what I should do, and who I should be with. I am divinely guided.

I tune up my inner knowing now, for I am moving through the shift with grace. I am a child of light and of energy, of sound, frequency and color. I am loved, and I am protected every step of the way.

And now, dear ones, we bring a keeper of the pyramids to you, one who will sit at the very top of this double pyramid. Ask this one to present itself to you so you can see what this one looks like. Ask this one to touch you, so you will know what the feeling is—a knock on the head, a sneeze, a squeeze on the hand, a feeling in the heart, breathlessness.

Dear one, when you need to cleanse your aura or protect yourself, your keeper on the pyramids will alert you. And if you feel you cannot receive this message, simply choose to do this cleansing every day. Option 2 is to give the keeper of the pyramids a sign. Tell this beautiful one, this loving one what you will do when you call upon him or her.

Indeed, the golden pyramid of cleansing and healing and love, and the green pyramid is for cleansing out your auric field and every chakra, and for cutting the cords of all negativities and lifting you higher. The keeper of the pyramids is with you now and forever.

Come back into your bodies a little, feeling this light, and we will lift you, indeed, in that which is known as ascension. Very good, you are there. Just lift with, "Yes."

We are connecting you to your soul's path, integrating what your soul wanted your personality to do in this lifetime, and we are releasing all resistance and all fear to living the life of your dreams, of your higher self, of your soul.

I Am the light of God. I am love, and I am freedom. I am cleansed and I am whole. I vibrate peace wherever I go. I vibrate joy, for I Am the very nucleus of my universe. I Am wholeness, and from me and my consciousness, I project healing now. And so it is. And so I let it be.

Bring yourself very easily, slowly and lovingly back into your body. You will feel very, very light. It is all right. Take your time. Take your time. And when you are ready—there is no rush—thank yourself, thank your guides and angels. Remember all of them, and when you are ready, think, *Feet.* Send your grounding energy into Mother Earth, and come back.

We want you to know, dear ones, that the reason for cleansing is there will become more of what you might call a 'bombardment.' We do not wish to use words that scare you.

You have heard of disharmonious energies. You have heard of—we are going to use a common word—'psychic attacks.' This does not mean it has to be conscious.

If anyone is angry at you and thinks angry thoughts of you because you are opening to the light, you will simply feel it more. That is why you must cleanse yourself.

And you, likewise, dear ones, if you are angry at someone else and think angry thoughts at them, you are sending them a psychic attack. Release it, let it go. Remember the words: "God forgive them; they do not know what they do."

Have good boundaries, love yourself, cleanse yourself, protect yourself. Take care of your aura, your energy field. Be good to yourself, be happy, and cleanse.

So, we do this cleansing because there will be so much clearing on your planet that people will not know they are releasing so much…and because of your sensitivity, you may get bombarded. The more sensitive you are—and you know who you are—the more frequently you must cleanse your aura, so you can be grounded in your body to do the good work you are here to do, and to love from joy and harmony and wholeness, not despair and confusion, because you do not know what you have picked up.

Cleanse yourself and you will be fine. Start this shift by taking care of your energy body. Be proactive, know who you are, and be it. Be it. And be in love. Be in joy. Thank you. And so it is.

9
Earth Predictions and How to Overcome Them

Indeed, beloveds, hello. We are here in full force, indeed, and allow yourselves to know this is Orion, and I do have with me all you have invited, and then some. Know, indeed, you have at least one guardian angel. We are going to lift your frequency slowly, easily, gracefully, but surely into the higher realms.

We spoke to you that the first step, the first stage of your becoming very aware of preparing for this shift that you are now, may we say, enjoying, is to remember the words "frequency and focus" You are increasing in frequency, and what you focus on is going to be manifested more easily and more quickly. Of course, there is a flip side to that coin. You want to train yourself to focus on what you want, not on what you are worrying about. So, dear ones, the shift is a good thing in that you are becoming highly, highly creative.

We would like to continue with letting you know your guardian angels are around you right now.

Everyone has a minimum of two or three guardian angels, and it is not just because you need them; it is because you have earned them. The more service a human being does for your planet Earth, the more guardian angels you will acquire. The more desire you have in your heart to accumulate spiritual help, the more spiritual help you will have.

Now, why do some of you desire spiritual help and yet see it, find it, feel it not? There is simply another belief is at hand and blocking you…and this is a belief of perhaps whether you deserve it or whether it is even real.

You see, beloveds, there is very deep, deep programming in your psyche, and, dear ones, you are the enlightened ones. So we say to you, if there is deep programming in your psyche, how much deeper is it in mass consciousness? It is frightening, is it not? Frightening to think about what the masses need to overcome in order to jump the hurdle to the other side of the fence.

We would like to use the analogy you often use: "The grass is greener on the other side of the fence." Well, in this case, it is true. Yes, in this case, it is true. The grass is greener, and you know it.

We would like you to know your knowledge is a tool in your preparation to move gracefully through the shift. Allow yourself to collect and accumulate more knowledge, and remember, frequency and focus and knowledge.

We would like to make you aware of some of the things that are actually happening in the third dimension, and that you, the essence of you, is not limited to the third dimension, but your focus is on it, you see. So step 2 is refocusing on who you really are and choos-ing to identify with who you really are. Re-identify.

You know how we love the words: "take a vacation." Allow yourself to enjoy recreation. Recreate. So in this instance, you are recreating yourself as you refocus on what is true, not on the fantasy or the dream of the third dimension.

In a sense, you might say you have been trapped, held captive by a captive audience called your mind, or your ego and agreement. You have been well programmed by parents, teachers and peers and other people from whom you desire approval. It is now time to be your own authority. It is now time to truncate the unnecessary opinions of people you love. Can you do that? Can you still love them and not need their agreement? Can you? Dear ones, if you can still love without approval, you are halfway home free.

There is a portion of your human mind that wants to defend itself, and worse, wants to attack those who do not agree with who and what you think you are. Well, you are *not* who you *think* you are. You are God, and there is no limit on that much love, is there?

So we say to you, learn to let go of all this judgment and let go of the polarities of right and wrong, good and bad, hot and cold, high and low. Allow yourself to live more in the impermanent nature of the God I Am.

The God-self is in a constant state of change. So whatever is going on now, it will change from one polarity to the next. It is only your mind that wants you to believe it is right or wrong.

The mind, very, very rarely, only if you are in the channeled state, will allow you a moment of grace, of equality, of unity and balance and harmony. That is what you are truly seeking in this shift. You are seeking the state of harmony and peace. You can do this.

This is why we came. We are the energy of light from another universe. Yes, we have a frequency that is at a higher beat, you might say, and through the physical universal law of entrainment, we can lift you to a higher frequency, to the degree you are willing to do so.

All you need to do is think, *Yes, I wish this,* and then join us through your focus. And as you focus on love, as you offer love, and as you respond from love, you will automatically lift into it, into higher and higher states of bliss. Bliss is the Kingdom of Heaven.

You are not bound by your physical body, unless you believe yourself to be. You are not bound by physical circumstances, unless you believe yourself to be. And now let us tell you the kicker: The reason you are attracting your challenges is so you can demonstrate to yourself once and for all, "I can overcome." Are you ready? We know you are ready or you would not have attracted them.

How can you overcome? Do not believe in them, and do not believe you are human. Do not believe in your rational mind.

We want you this next week to laugh more, play more, and rest more. Can you do that for yourselves? Laugh more, play more, and rest more.

If you do, you will be developing the other side of your brain, and you will be relaxing this unnecessary grip you have on making things make sense. If you are trying to make the world make sense, you are trapped. You are trapped, and you will not ascend.

What we are wanting you to accept does not make sense, and it never will. Are you ready? Are you really ready to fly with the angels? Well then, you must let go of this mind that says, "It does not make sense, I cannot believe it." If you cannot believe it, you will not fly.

Just like that spaceship in the film *Star Wars* with Yoda and Luke. Do you really believe in the Force? Do you really believe you are one with God? Do you really believe you are more than your body? If you do, you will ascend. You will poof, you might say, from this place like quantum physics. Like the atoms that poof from one place to the next. And it just will not make sense. Are you ready? We know you are.

Now there are arguments going on within some of your minds—yes, no…yes, no—like a ping-pong ball, "I'm ready, I'm not ready, I'm ready, I'm not ready." This is where your focus comes in. You can choose your focus; and as you choose to hold your focus on love, truth, God, light and I Am divine consciousness, you will retrain your own mind.

It is programming. You are building synapses in your mind, and there is a kind of physical physics involved with this as well as free will. So, choose to hold your focus on love and allow the frequency of love to lift you.

And now educate yourself a bit and let us tell you about what is going on in the third dimension, so you can know and choose once again. There is a physical shift going on, and the reason there is a physical shift going is because there is a shift in your consciousness.

"As within, so without." It is not the other way around— as without, so within. No, no, no. "As within, so without." So what it looks like 'without' is that you are moving in your solar system through space, and, of course, you know better than to think you are the only living beings in this universe upon universe upon universe.

There are many beings, and we would wish for you to know you are a beautiful race, and we are here because you *are* loving and you wish to grow and know in all of your most magnificent parts that you *are* divine. And we have heard this S.O.S., if you will, and we come because we are your brothers and sisters in light.

So, dear ones, we wish to enlighten you. Your Earth, this mass of flesh and blood for the body is a larger organism, it is alive, and we encourage you to love your Mother Earth.

It is moving through space, and it is moving through the Milky Way. It is moving through star systems, and as it does, it is meeting up with other gravitational force-fields, other influences.

Astrology comes into play in your life until you realize you are more powerful than the forces that are put upon you, and choose a higher thought. Then you can begin to live at the highest echelon of any astrological predictions.

And so this is what we are asking you to do now, where your Earth is the subject. You have an opportunity to first learn to overcome any psychic's predictions, if you do not like them. You have an opportunity to overcome any astrological predictions, if you choose a higher thought, and you also have an opportunity to overcome what is coming towards your Earth if you choose to.

We have been talking to you about ascension for 16 years, and it is now of utmost importance, if you would like to move through the shift gracefully, and if you would like to live in this body.

We have talked to you about how some will go to the left and some will go to the right, some will move towards love and some will move towards fear. It is time to choose sides. Not that it is a competition.

It is in you, this competition. Who are you really? If you know who you are, you will choose love every time and every moment, and we want you to know in all of your challenges, choose love. In all of your thoughts, choose love. In all of your pain, and all of your emotions. It is good to have your emotions. It is teaching you to feel what is true and real, and move towards love.

Ask yourself, "Do I need to suffer and how can I move into love now? Do I need to suffer? No. How can I move into love now?" There will always be an answer to that question.

Will you listen and will you act? The choice is yours. It is always yours, and no one else can help you with this choice. You may even be in a relationship, and one of you may choose to the left and one of you to the right. This is not a group choice. It is up to you.

So, dear ones, we invite you to reconsider your commitment to your spiritual work now, and we know you are doing this. You may not *know* you are doing this to such a degree, but you are reading this book, so that is the physical manifestation of your subconscious urge to bring the light into the dawning of a new age of enlightenment in this physical body.

And that is why you are here. You chose this incarnation, you know? You chose to be a master. Yodas all are you, not Lukes. Yodas. And we celebrate that in you.

So, your Earth plane, your Earth, your globe, this is a global shift, you know. It is not just your world, not just your city, not just your nation, it is global, it is moving, and as it moves, it comes into contact with other force-fields, and it becomes susceptible to things such as weather pattern changes.

We know this sounds frightening. We are letting you know what is going on, because we know you are curious. But remember, you are not your body, and therefore you are not isolated or limited to the third dimension.

Your responsibility, your mission, should you choose to accept it, is to ascend every day, to lift your frequency so that you can lift out of the third dimension into reality with your body where you can live in Heaven on Earth, where you can live with those who also believe, who also know who they are.

So, your Earth is on a timetable, as it were, and yes, it has been predicted. You know it has been predicted, not just by the Mayan calendar. The date is December 21, 2012 when the Mayan calendar ends, predicted by the Incas and the Egyptians, and even Einstein once brought it up in one of his dialogues.

Do you know your government, even in about 1984 and again in the early 1990s, talked about an unidentified, large mass was moving towards the Earth? In the 1980s, it was about 32 billion light years away, and then in the 1990s it was 7 billion. So it is on target in an orbit, you might say.

It is possible that you will live to know two suns. That is how large it is. And whether it hits your Earth or hits your sun is yet to be seen, but it will shake things up. So, it is going to be flying in an orbit. How close it comes is yet to be seen, but it will come within a 'force-field,' that will affect your planet in such a way that the oceans will rise and fall greatly, earthquakes will happen, there will be changes in weather patterns and people will be very afraid.

You must choose now. You have had all these little worries, which you think are big, but they are nothing. You are learning how to hold your focus and your frequency.

You are the saviors. This is the Second Coming, and you are the one. And that is the responsibility. This is the Second Coming, and you are the one to hold your focus on what you know is true—that you are the light of God. And if there are enough of you, the world will lift.

This is not a death; it is a rebirth, a transcendence. It is the end of life as you have known it. And if you do your loving, loving homework, you will not know of this devastation.

There are Web sites out there, including one called NetBotz. You can look for it. It is a way that those who are in the know have used the Internet to research mass consciousness of your planet.

This has been going on for about 20 years, and these brilliant scientists used the technology of your Internet to predict the tsunami. Totally right on. The very day. It was used to predict the storm called Katrina. It has been used to exactly predict to the day, and it has predicted December 21, 2012.

And so there is change. And it is big, and it is coming. And we say that you have come here because you are angels, because you have raised your beautiful, loving, angelic wings and said, "I can lift this frequency, and I will do it." This is part of your passion and your mission.

So we say to you lovingly, "The Earth does not need to end." Your governments are well aware of this. Every government is, but they are not alerting you. They do not want to. Can you imagine the mass consciousness fear?

At this stage, not everyone can be saved, but your civilization will continue. You can assist in changing everything.

So, there is a coming, a parting, you might say, of what once was the Red Sea—some going to the left, some going to the right. Why not choose to go the right way? Choose love, choose to do the ascension, pray, laugh, and love every moment you can. Smile at people, teach them to love, teach them how to respond.

Do not react in anger. Do not defend nor attack. You are the light of God. Why are you attacking? Why are you defending yourself? Have you forgotten? This is not the time to forget. This is the time to remember better.

So every challenge has been your soul's effort to help you to remember that you are the light of God, and now is the time to really, really dig your heels in.

We do not give you this message so that you promote fear. If you promote fear, you are using this message the wrong way. This is education.

You have been curious. You asked, "Is something coming?" It is coming, but the only reason it is coming is that it is a shift in consciousness. It is the rebirth. It is the time for a new world for those who wish to ascend.

And so, you are the ones, and what can you do to help? You can love yourselves. You can find that you are worth giving three minutes or fifteen minutes a day to placing your hands on Mother Earth and saying, "I love you." Hold an animal, "I love you." Hold a friend and hug them, "I love you." And put your hands up into the mirror and gaze into your image and say, "I love you. I forgive you." Everywhere you can go, "I forgive you, I forgive you, I forgive you."

Let go of your pettiness. You are more than that. You are the light of God, and you are what the world has been waiting for. Any other thought is too small for you now. It is time to choose.

So we invite you to lift your frequency through prayer and laughter, through ascension and loving every single day, and then, yes then, you will be doing your part.

Remember, focus, frequency, education, and re-identification. *I am the light of God. I am bigger than circumstance. I am more than my body. I am the beginning of new life, and I lovingly and willingly accept this mission now, and I will do this by re-identifying myself with light and power and miracles.*

And, beloveds, in so doing, you will ascend. You will absolutely ascend. You will lift your body, and you can take as many as three or four others with you as you strengthen this, out of harm's way and into the new tomorrow.

So, we thank you. We thank you for listening. But more than that, we thank you for taking the necessary action. We love you. We are always here with you. You are not alone.

Now you are more aware that you are the light of God, and a host of angels and star beings go with you, and we are here to assist you every time you call upon us. Every single time. So, we thank you, and we lovingly let it be. And so it is.

100

———

ASCENSION

Part III

ORION CHANNELS

102

———

ASCENSION

I Am the Light of the Oneself
June 18, 2007

Beloved angels of light, know indeed that you are the angels who fill this room, and we are delighted to be with you. You are ascending. You will become the ascended masters that others down the road will talk to. Yes, you are masters in training.

Many of you carry the light, I Am, at a conscious level now in your heart, and soon to be on your sleeve. And what this means is, you will come forward as a teacher of the I Am consciousness and awareness.

You see, beloved angels, you come into this room this evening not just on happenstance, but as a divine assignment. You have been told at levels of your own awareness that perhaps you have forgotten you have a mission, a holy mission, a divine purpose. And this life you are living is not by accident.

Why indeed, dear ones, everything that has ever occurred to you, the good, the bad, the ugly and everything in between, has come to help design you to be all that you can be in this lifetime, so you can serve on this planet Earth in the greatest way possible.

Your planet is spiraling forward so quickly now it is, indeed, beginning to quiver and shake on its axis, and it is heading towards the year 2012 when there will be a wonderful, divine explosion of energy. It really does depend a lot on you and all the other Lightworkers what will happen to your beautiful planet between now and then.

You look around yourselves and you see all the crises. There are crises of every kind in every area of your life, and yet we recognize that you, beloved, yes you, are quite capable of recognizing you can have it all, and some of you in this room or reading this are about divining that. We call it 'divining' because you are consciously co-creating with God to have a life that is congruent with your higher self. You are already divining a life of your dreams.

When you come here for these channelings, you, at a conscious or unconscious level, are connecting with a very high frequency of love that helps you to create for yourself a better life.

This voice that calls itself Orion, I who come forward as a teacher unto you, as a spirit guide, wish for you to know the energy that comes through comes through not only giving information and guidance, but comes through as an energy transmission. Thus, this makes this evening different from what you would call just a channeling or a linear experience of listening to information. This is light infusion. This light is transmitted to you, and at the level of your willingness and readiness to receive it, begins an awakening process in you.

Some of you have heard of energetic transmissions or awakenings before. This is the awakening of the divine. I wish for you to know, dear ones, this is what is occurring. When you come to this group meeting, there is this energy infusion that moves into your aura and awakens the light I Am in you, and you begin to align more and more with your higher values, with integrity, honesty and balance, with self-love, humanity, compassion and forgiveness, and on and on.

Thus, when you are in the world of third dimension and have a situation of crisis, and we know you all do, you think twice about reacting from your unconscious responses of fear, and in thinking twice, you think just enough to reconsider, *Who am I really and what am I living for?*

These are wonderful questions, beloveds, and you would not think them if you were not beginning to vibrate at a higher frequency, and you would not be in this room this evening if you were not vibrating at a higher frequency, and thus assisting the stabilizing of your Earth plane and preparing her for the ascension that is coming.

It is happening, but it will be greatly increased around the year 2012 and moving into 2020. There are a lot of ifs around the span of years between 12 and 20, thus this timetable is according to consciousness, the mass consciousness of the Earth. So what you do between now and 2012 is very important, and your being here and taking this light out into the world, into your little corner of the world, is not so little. It is very important.

Thus you come, and we feed you this light. It integrates into your light field, and you respond. You find yourself, indeed, opening your heart. Opening the heart may not always be easy, but if you choose to come back, if you choose to love, if you choose to be willing, it will open again.

Keep choosing love. When the thought of fear arises, we wish to give you a new thought to focus on, and this is what this evening is all about.

We notice that each week we are giving you a brief lesson. This week we wish you to take with you a thought, a mantra, if you will, for there is healing vibration in it. When you are faced with crisis in your life and you are tempted to respond with fear, pause and ask, "What do I do here?"

Take this thought with you, our dear angels of light: I am the light of the oneself. And that is all. You might break it down, if you will, into three portions. I am. I am the light. I am the light of the oneself.

We wish to remind you that everything is energy, or sound or frequency. You are energy. If you were to view yourself under a microscope, there would be nothing there. You vibrate according to your thoughts and your feelings, and your thoughts and your feelings are the result of your free will.

What choose you to focus on? What choose you to feel? It is your choice. Beloveds, you are not at the effect of your environment. You are not at the effect of other people, unless you believe you are, and then you have given your power away through your own free will. Bring it back. It is easy. How do you use your free will? You can have everything. You are creator god.

I am the light of the oneself. What does this mean? Know who you are and be free. This is important. This will change everything. In the hour of need, I am the light of the oneself. Bring this into your heart now, and let it vibrate with you. We wish for you to take this thought with you this week and the next and the next and the next, because it will change your life. Is that a good enough reason for the mind? We know the heart resonates with this.

It will change your life. And if it changes your life, it will change the lives of everyone whom you touch, because your aura touches their aura, and you cannot hide truth. Truth reveals itself, you know.

You have heard over and over again the saying: "Who you are speaks so loudly I can't hear what you're saying." People know who you are without your opening your mouth. It is obvious. Who are you?

If you do not know who you are, look around your life and see what you are mirroring back to yourself. That is your belief about who you are, but it is not truly who you are. You are beautiful, perfection, love, eternal, bliss, creativity, and that is why we very simply give to you this one mantra that carries a great deal of frequency—*I am the light of the oneself.*

We wish to keep it simple that you might remember it. Think it again—*I am the light of the oneself.* And this is all you need to do to change yourself this week.

Take this mantra and think it throughout your day when you find you might be in crisis or when you find you think of it, because you are energy, and because you can affect the energy with a thought.

The thought you take is empowered by the feeling and belief behind it. If you take this thought carelessly and just think it, it will be less effective than if you truly bring it into your heart and feel it and be it. Act as if, and it shall be. Allow it to become you, for it already is you.

Find the place in you that knows itself, and then from there speak this thought, silently or out loud. This is the living word, and when spoken with truth, its resonance will vibrate from you and heal you and your environment. *I am the light of the oneself.* This very short and simple, yet powerful statement can change the world.

We know it is very, very popular at this time in your society, and we are in harmony and agreement with it, to recognize the beautiful Law of Attraction, and yet what we would like to appeal to you about this Law of Attraction is the awareness of, "What you think is what you get, what you focus on is what you get," often applies to the third dimension, the world of form. More money, more health, more beauty, more stuff.

There is nothing wrong with stuff unless you believe that you *are* your stuff, unless you believe that the bliss of the Kingdom of Heaven comes from stuff. It is difficult for a rich man or woman to get to the Kingdom of Heaven. Why? Because, beloveds, once you have gotten some stuff, your mind will tell you that you need more stuff. All right, I need a bicycle, and now I need a car, and I got a Volkswagen and now I need a Mercedes and now I need a Lamborghini. You see how it goes on and on? The stuff must always improve itself for that part of the mind to convince itself that it is enough or happy. It becomes a game of collection.

How many people do you know who collect things? There is nothing wrong with collecting cups or spoons or cars, unless you believe that your identification of how good you are or how much bliss you can feel comes from your stuff. If you are playing that game, you are fooling yourself. That is the greatest error in thinking. Please do not stop there.

Allow yourself to use this Law of Attraction for feeling good, to include feeling all the way to the Kingdom of Heaven and needing nothing on the outside world to equate this feeling of peace and Heaven on Earth with. You are enough, you see.

We want you to enjoy your life, your human life. We want you to enjoy it, of course, but do not feel that the bliss you are looking for will be found in the world of form or you will miss it. That is all we are saying: That there is a power within you that is more beautiful than anything that is in the world. And it is in you.

Why, dear ones, do you not notice, let us say, when you go about your day and the day goes on and on you become weary or tired, and then you take a nap or you go to sleep at night and you awake refreshed? And oh, how good you feel. Does that not show you somewhat there is a power in you that refreshes and rejuvenates you? You are taking care of your physical body, but your spiritual body feels better, too.

And we would say to you, in your dream state, you may have good dreams and bad dreams, and you may ask, "What does this mean? and "Is this real?" And then you wake up to your third-dimensional reality and you may ask, "What does this mean?" and, "Is this real?" We tell you truly, neither is real. You are more than that. You are more than your mind.

So we invite you, solemnly and joyfully, to travel with us where the mind can never go, and that is home to the kingdom of light, to Heaven, if you will, to true bliss where nothing can destroy this.

All things in form may come and go, and you may indeed choose to enjoy them, but enjoy them knowing they come to pass. For this world of form is like the waves on an ocean—they rise and they fall—and the things in your world come and they go. Everything in your world, including your body, comes and goes.

If you stop your search there, you will be greatly confused and frustrated. That is not the point of your life. The point of your life is consciousness.

The point of your choosing this human incarnation is to awaken from this beautiful dream. The point of your life, your purpose, is to awaken or heal your consciousness to the only true bliss you can ever experience.

And then all things can be given unto you in the physical, and it will not matter. You will have freedom. You will know these things will come and go. You will, in a way, expect it.

You will not tell yourself, "Oh I have to hold onto this good thought, I have to hold onto this good feeling, I will lose this substance that has now come into my life."

You are creator god, and this arena called my life will see many forms of beauty come and go, and it will see disturbances come and go. But you, as the I Am, are choosing to witness it without becoming attached to it, without becoming afraid of it, without being at the effect of it, just witnessing it as if you are standing beside a beautiful river watching it flow, and forms are coming.

You see them coming and now they pass right in front of you, and you see them go. And you just watch, and enjoy the view. It is beautiful. But to the degree you become attached to any form, you will have pain. That is all. So we invite you to a higher level of experiencing life...and that is the life within yourself.

So you see, what you are witnessing right now is a wonderful opportunity to recognize that the nourishment of your spirit is the greatest thing you can choose to do with your time. Your meditations, your prayers, your channelings, your ascensions—the nourishing of your spirit allows you an avenue to eternal bliss.

Until you know who you are from direct experience, nothing will satisfy you or make you happy. You will continue to be a seeker of truth. But what we are all about is helping you to be a finder of truth.

So we offer to you the vibration of an incredibly powerful mantra. And as you feel it, and as you think it, it will begin to influence you at the level of frequency. From the very core of your body, you will begin to change.

You see, this sound does not just come forth from your mouth, it comes forth from within you. Deep within you. And not just from your body, but also your aura, this mind/heart/body complex. But it does move up from your third chakra, which is known as your power chakra. It starts with a frequency.

We would equate this to creation. There is this that is unformed, and this chakra begins this frequency of sound, and then it comes up to your heart and gains compassion and momentum. Then it comes up to your throat and it gains here at the throat the recognition of self and identification. Then as you speak it, it carries the frequency of coming into form, you see. It starts deep within you, and as it comes up through the chakras and is spoken, it is the living word. As you speak it, it becomes you.

So do not worry if you do not feel it yet. Just choose to not identify with the worry. Choose to identify with the self. I am light. *I am the light of the oneself.* That is all.

We ask you, for you, through you, to perhaps consider taking this mantra with you for a long time, until perhaps one day, a day of your own choosing, a most beautiful, auspicious day, that mantra is witness to the self awakening in you. You see as we look at you, we do not see God in you—we see God as you, and we with you are waiting for that day, that moment, when that realization quakes your being, you see.

That is the big change that is coming, the grand ascension. And if you awaken, then this Earth plane of yours can ascend. You are holding this frequency for all.

This day of ascension is coming very soon now, and we are working with you and preparing you for this. Of course, you, to the degree of your willingness, are working with us or procrastinating until you gain enough recognition that this is true. This truth may present itself in your world as a frightening experience, because unfortunately most human beings do not respond to doing inside work until something frightening happens to them, and then they sit up and take notice. Usually that is why you have crises in your life. It is to get your attention.

So, beloveds, the sooner you just go ahead and go within, the sooner you will experience who you are…and then nothing outside you can scare you again.

Why, indeed, everyone who comes to Betsy-Morgan asking questions has some point of unhappiness they wish relief from. The answer to every question can come from the answer to: "Who are you, and what truly is your purpose?"

So we answer that with one statement we offer to you wrapped in love—*I am the light of the oneself.* That is the answer, and that is your purpose. You are the light. And as you know who you are, that purpose awakens in you, and you will have no other ability but to live that purpose.

For as you open, that which you call chakras, or vortexes of energy, open to light and are fed directly, and your inner gifts become exposed, known, and offered. It does not even matter what they are. They are good and they are love, and your world is waiting.

They can be gifts of healing, of mediumship, of helping lost souls move into the light, of seeing into the future, of love and bliss and service. It can be uniquely yours. This world is waiting for you. Wake up this day and know who you are.

You are loved, deeply, deeply loved. And we are with you. We are with you now and always. There are many, many angels and spirit guides with you, dear angels, and we are waiting for that moment when you say, "I am ready."

Akhenaten
June 25, 2007

Beloved beings of light, it is I, Akhenaten. This is a
name that comes from an energy likened to Orion, but
as if, even for your ability to understand, as if a father
unto this one, a larger sphere of influence, a higher
one, and we come as a congregation, a vortex of energy,
many energies pooled into one source, to lift you even
higher this evening.

This is a grand evening. This particular evening,
where we have come perhaps, you might say, uninvited,
but well intentioned, to come in with agreement with
your soul to lift your frequency to the heights it might
go.

When your frequency or energy form, your aura,
your true self, is lifted, this allows an opening at the
top of your very being, which is unseen by your eye,
into a higher vortex of energy, and there is communication and communion. When your frequency lifts,
you begin to align with higher light, and at an uncon-

scious level, begin to become very, very aware of who you truly are.

As you move around in your human form, there is an identification that comes from the level of the personality, or the ego, that says, "I am human and therefore limited." You move around with the context of *I am human and limited.* There are many belief systems, usually negative, that are associated with being only human. These belief systems usually keep you bound to the world and at the effect of all the consequences you attract in your life.

What we are doing in this aspect of ascension throughout the remainder of this healing process called channeling is upping your energy vortex for the entire session, for you are ready and you are capable of this…and it is time. This frequency lifting will cleanse you out, leaving you open at the top for the availability of your will to choose to fill it with a golden light and a halo, and then silver light, and then a light blue, to connect you all the way up to the Kingdom of Heaven, or the All That Is, to connect you to higher awareness.

This is a very unusual evening, very power-packed. We want you to recognize the importance of yourself as energy, as light.

Last week we gave you a very powerful mantra—*I am the light of the oneself*—and we asked you to repeat that mantra, which some of you did, and we appreciate that. A few of you repeated it a few times during the week, but most of you thought of it and let it go. It is all right, for it is in you. It has planted a seed as light, as frequency. It is in you. But we refer to this because this is the truth we are building upon in this particular session in this evening.

This vortex was left last week with a thought form, and it awaits you in this group this evening to build upon that. If you were here, that which is in you as seed thought is being utilized in this higher intention, that this vortex of light lifts itself, indeed, into the light I Am of the highest consciousness you can reach this evening.

You are light. You are energy. You are energy, and as you touch upon or come into close contact with a higher energy form, your frequency ups itself. There is a spiritual law in this universe that says the highest energy wins. This is a law that is true everywhere.

It is difficult for your mind to begin to comprehend a world without end. Where does the universe end? If you think about it, it goes and goes and then does it end? If it does not end, how can you begin to perceive that which is eternal? This is very difficult for your mind, but there is a part of your Self, with a capital "S", that accepts it, that knows it, and that can utilize this information and build upon it. This is where we connect this evening, with that Self, with that light and with that truth.

So, we lift you in frequency, we increase your vibration, and this is done by coming in and offering to you, through invitation, that you engage with us for the purpose of lifting. This lifting will result in a practical way in your life as harnessing love—love as light and love as energy, love as health and healing, love as purely loving.

We know you all love the feeling of falling in love, rising in love, perhaps being in love, and yet we know this part of the personality called the ego will eventually find fault with the beloved. And then the ego, if focused upon long enough, will find enough fault where in time you may wish to change lovers, because you want the feeling of falling in love again.

There is a kind of addiction to that feeling. That is all right; it is just that it is a no-win game, because it goes on and on. When you have an addiction to falling in love, then it results in the need for change on the outside, you see.

What we are talking about is the change that is total and complete, and it occurs on the inside, on the inner, where you fall in love with self, with the oneself. It is a different kind of falling in love and does not require changing anything on the external. For you begin to fall in love with a realization that nothing on the external counts anyway, that on the external is only a projection of that which is going on in the internal.

But it goes beyond that. It is a continuum of a feeling of bliss when you do not need to change anything on the outside in order to feel the truth of your being. This is truly rising in love, and this is the reason or the context in which we are operating, that we lift you to a higher vortex, to a higher frequency, so, as you live your life pretending you are a human being, you will not fall short of the glory of the God within yourself, but rather you will have a greater sense of humor about your life.

You see, it is only those who have more fear that fail to see the humor in life. When you are without fear, when you are aligning with love in your higher self, you are very, very powerful indeed, and you find yourself laughing a lot. You find humor, because you do not believe in what is happening, you do not validate it, you do not give agreement to it and you are not attached.

To the degree you are attached to outcomes, you will suffer, that is all. It is not wrong. It is only a lesson. To the degree you are attached to outcomes, you are believing that who you are is limited to the third dimension.

Oh, beloved beings, you are so much more than this third dimension your body occupies. You are limitless love, limitless I Am consciousness. You are totally unlimited.

As we lift you in this way, you will begin to explore, you will begin to experience, you will begin to know, and you will begin to express the expanded nature of your true being.

You do not need to be a limited human being. It is only a belief. It is only a belief you were born with that has been anchored into your mind, and you are not your mind. You are beginning to supersede the need for the limited mind, and you are becoming very, very creative.

Indeed, you are harnessing the processes of your own imagination. We say you are limited only by your imagination. Stretch it a bit. Pretend. Daydream. Let yourself run wild and run free. If you imagine it, you can achieve it. It is not the processes of your mind that set you free, but of your imagination, and releasing all of the beliefs that have held you back.

There is a whole new world out there, and we mean that. Not a whole new world as if you could travel to Jamaica or a beautiful tropical island. We are talking about a whole new world with vibration and frequency. You see, the world you see is a frequency, and as you increase your frequency, you will move into a higher dimension and will experience more beauty, more bliss, more joy, more love, and those outcomes you are so insistent upon having will be more beautiful.

But you will not be doing it for the outcome; you will be doing it for God's sake. You will simply be lifting because you know inherently the truth of your being is Heaven, is home, is truth.

We know, our beloved beings of light, what you want more than anything is, quite simply, more God, or you would not be here this evening. We know the mind does not even know what that means, and yet you are willing. You are willing to go where very few human beings are willing to go. You are willing to go into the unknown, because you love, because you love God, and your mind does not even know what that means.

Welcome to this new world. You are now entering a new dimension where your future is unwritten. We hand you paper and pen, and we hand you a bushel basket of love and light. It is a new world. Your future is waiting. You can have anything you want.

You are going to get a new script now. We encourage you after this evening to keep it open at the top, as you have heard before. You have a new life script. You have asked for this. You have prayed for this. You have longed for this. It is yours.

God has given you everything. The reason you have not accepted everything, quite simply, is because of your resistance to do so...which is called belief systems. The belief might be: I am not worthy, or, I am not ready, or, I am afraid, or, I am afraid of the change, or, I don't know how to receive that much love. You know those thoughts, and many of them are unconscious. You may not know them consciously, but your thoughts are creating your world.

So with this huge frequency lifting, we simply lift you out of the mire of your past, of those negative thoughts that have gotten you into a rut.

Are you ready? Are you truly ready for the fast track? Are you ready to enjoy your life?

Are you ready to give up what has been draining your energy? Are you ready to let it go? That is all we ask of you. What would you have? The future is yours. And every moment is yours.

We know some of you have this storyline: "It will all work out in the end. It will all work out in the end, and the price that I pay is worth it." Oh this is a sad, sad storyline.

We hate to tell you so, because we know it is a very nice storyline, and it has gotten you past many people and many situations, where you will say, "It is going to work out in the end." You do not need to wait till the end. The journey, my friends, is as important as the end.

You are living a spiritual journey. Every day and every moment of your journey can be filled with laughter. How would it feel to you to be laughing your way through the day? Would that not be delightful? Would that not be a new option, a new paradigm?

This is what we offer to you, and all you need to do is be willing. When you awaken in the morning, all you need to do is identify your passion. Be honest about it. Speak what is your passion, what is your joy, what you want. Speak what you want and live from it.

We will get you there, but we cannot keep you there, you see, because we cannot take your free will. We are giving you a jumpstart, a booster start, like a booster rocket, but we cannot take your free will. It is yours.

We wish to tell you a story, and it is a very true story, and you will relate to this for it could be your story.

Once upon a time, there was a man we shall call Harry. Harry was in love with Charlotte. He adored her, but he was afraid he might get rejected.

From a distance he longed to meet her. And finally, one day he did meet her, and they seemed to have a nice conversation.

He knew where she was hanging out, and he went there the next day and talked with her again and it was wonderful.

Harry loved Charlotte and wanted to get to know her more, but the more he got to know her, the more afraid he became she would know him and reject him, so he withdrew from contacting Charlotte.

He waited many months and then one day he thought, *I must see her, I must.* He called her, invited her out for what you call a date, and to his surprise she said, "Yes." He was very excited about this opportunity. He worried about it all day long.

As he drove to her house, he thought, *What if she doesn't like me? What if she changed her mind? What if she doesn't laugh at my jokes? What if?* But he did find himself walking up to the door, and as he knocked, she actually opened the door and greeted him, and it felt to him that she was happy, but he was still afraid.

Charlotte reached out and handed him a book as a gift, telling him, "This is one of my favorite books. I hope you enjoy it, too."

Harry escorted her to his car, and they sat in the car, and he put the book in the backseat, because he was so focused on his fear that she would not like him. They went on the date and she laughed as his jokes. But as he took her home that night, he was so filled with fear, as he said, "Goodnight," he did not lean over to kiss her goodnight. He shook her hand, thanked her politely, and walked off, saying, "That was so frightening, I don't think I'll call her again."

A year went by, and he heard through the grapevine that Charlotte had married, and he was very unhappy. Then another year and another year until ten years went by, and he heard through the grapevine that Charlotte had passed away.

The friend that called him to give him the bad news said, "I am so sorry about your friend, and by the way, would you like this book she gave you? You loaned it to me a few weeks after your date."

Harry said, "Yes, I will retrieve the book. I don't know why."

Harry's friend said, "Well there's an inscription in this book."

Harry said, "Read it to me," and his friend said, "Oh no, no, no, it's way too intimate. You should have this book."

Harry drove over, picked up the book, drove off and sat under a cool shade tree as he tentatively opened the book to read what the inscription, written ten years ago on that one date, had said. And as he opened that book, with tears in his eyes, it said: *Harry, it's now or never. Charlotte.*

So, beloveds, with the greatest of love, it's now or never. This is your life. This is your opportunity, and it is your free will.

You know your life is so busy. We know your life is busy. We watch you running around. Have you ever seen ants when they find a piece of food and they have this line going to the left and one to the right? Some ants are going to the food and some are taking it back home, and on and on.

We see you like that—hurry, hurry, hurry—and we see your lives full of activities. Quite entertaining. Quite dramatic.

For these activities to be seen as really advantageous, we offer to you two questions: 1) What are the activities you are choosing to fill up your life? and 2) What is the attitude in which you live these activities? What is the attitude?

Yes, your life is a journey, and every second of every day it is your choice to be happy or to be sad. It is not anyone else's choice; it is not anyone else's responsibility, and for Heaven's sake, it is not your past. Get over that.

Stop fearing your future. You are more spiritually mature than that. If you live fully in this present moment with love, there is no future. Do you hear us? If you live fully in this moment with love, there is no future. You do not 'futurize,' you do not worry, because you are too preoccupied with being happy. Happy people do not worry about their future. No. And you are those.

You are the light of the one true self. You are the saviors. But how do you save a world? One person at a time. We only ask that you save just one...yourself.

Beloved angels of light, truly it is now or never. You will never get this opportunity again. Choose life.

So, we lift you for joy. We lift you for love. We lift you for redemption. We lift you for your freedom. We lift you for your happiness.

This life of yours can be everything you want it to be. You are the leaders. You are the light of the one true self. You are the light of God. You are the hope. So live your life as if it counts, because it does. Your life is not an accident. You are meant to be here.

You have a divine purpose, and that purpose is to set yourself free and really, really live. Do not believe in the fearful thoughts of your mind. Those thoughts will stop you from jumping. Jump. Do not think. Jump. Jump before you can think, and feel your freedom into being. When you jump, we assure you, you will fly. You will fly with us.

Heaven is a state of mind, and it is your free will to choose it. It is your choice, and it is but one choice away.

So, dear ones, we love you. We have come from heavens above, from other dimensions, indeed from beyond the beyond, and we are still one with you, and we still love you. You are precious, and you are worth it, or we would not have come. You are worth it. You are everything, and this is your life. Do not waste it. It is a beautiful, beautiful gift, and a fabulous, fabulous opportunity to jump. We thank you, beloveds. We love you.

* * *

I wish to introduce myself. My name is Akhenaten, son of Ra, father of Abraham, co-regent with Metatron. You may see a pyramid of light, for there is a great golden pyramid in this room, and you may feel one in your third eye.

There is an anointing, as an initiation, that is occurring for you in this group, and we thank you. You were called, and you responded. And that is all there is—to listen and to respond to that higher self. We thank you.

It is now your turn to move into the world, and let your energy initiate a wave, like a wave upon the ocean, a wave upon the sea of humanity. Let your light change the world, your world. That is all, let your light change your world. You are most effective.

The world you see in form is not the point. The world of form is not the point, it is the inner world you have come to receive, that you acknowledge by your presence this evening, that you celebrate collectively, that you open to individually. Let this light that enters your energy field change you in the ways you wish to change yourself. This is the gift. And we thank you. We thank you, beautiful beings of light. We thank you. And so it is.

128

———

ASCENSION

How to Integrate the New Energy
July 9, 2007

Beings of light, we have come to bring you song and have come to bring you joy.

This is a combination this evening of Orion and Akhenaten, and we come with messages of love and peace.

We are joining the worlds of ancient and new, and we are bringing light-encoded information to many of you who were in Egypt at that time of enlightenment into this arena, to bring information of understanding and acceptance of that which occurred before.

In the next hundred years, there will come enlightenment about what did occur in the Egyptian lands, and not everything, in fact not much, of what actually happened has been transcribed for you to hear and understand.

There was in the ancient of days much connection between the star beings, the Atlanteans, the star beings and the Egyptian pyramid builders, and many were star-seeded in that day and had combinations of energy, so you might say.

We are coming right now to broadcast to you in this moment, in this hour great energy of connecting you to your Egyptian lifetimes, and those of you who were there, those of you who were light-encoded can now begin to open the vastness of the reservoir of light within you to release this information that has been stored in your DNA and is ready to release, to be made known by the world at large.

Many of you will set up Web sites and broadcast this information, and many of you will put this information on that which we love called My Space. We love that term. We also see some of you writing manuscripts, others of you speaking, others of you drawing and others of you teaching, but this will be released into the world.

In the next 100 years or so, you will see enlightenment once again hitting your planet. It is time, as you know, to turn things around, and it is turning quite quickly, is it not? This has been termed 'turning on its axis, turning upside down.' Your world, your life, you, turning upside down. You are seeing many symbols in your world that this is indeed occurring. Change is in the air, and it is good.

We are broadcasting to you energy from long ago to awaken that which has been stored in you, waiting to awaken now. What you know, please share. You will have come from different eras in time and space. You will have different information to share. You will have different gifts to share. But this is the harvest, the gathering, the time of great sharing, and it is the time to give that gift, that gift of knowledge, that gift of knowing.

So, there is this that is opening in you, there is what is called the third eye in you, and this is opening and broadcasting information. Once we spoke this word, 'third eye,' you may now be feeling a pain, for a light is now being emanated from us to that point in you.

You may feel it from time to time as you continue to open over the next three months or so, especially those of you who have prepared and are willing and ready to do of this work.

There is a great light that is bombarding your Earth plane right now, and it will pick up speed, especially over the next two weeks or so. We suggest to you every day, and we have been suggesting, have we not, to do the ascension, which is the agreement of your willingness meeting our station, your willingness to lift in frequency to connect with a higher frequency, so this light I Am is instated once again in your consciousness at a very deep, moving, creative level. It is the awakening, and it is cause in your life and cause for your planet Earth.

For the past fifteen years, we have been saying, "Ascension, ascension, ascension," and encouraging you to relax and ask your friends in the stars, your friends in spirit, to assist you in lifting your frequency by simply asking. It is done to the degree you are willing and ready in every moment you ask.

We will now explain more for you what this means. When you say, "Yes," we are on call. You say, "Yes," and you have dominion over your kingdom, over your own energy field, over your aura, over your consciousness. When you say, "Yes," it is a very powerful statement to the god within the self of you, and it is lift-off time, you might say.

It is as if you are turning a knob—more speed, more light, more power, if you please, and molecules and atoms begin to jump around and bump around. There is this release then into your energy field and into that which is outside your energy field of which you do not need anymore, of who you are not anymore, and who you are not is negative beliefs. Who you are not is your past. Who you are not is your fear.

What happens is, you start to change radically, and you start to change so radically that some of you may feel a bit out of body, or disconnected or you may even begin to feel a little bit crazy. We know this is the last thing you want to feel—crazy or silly—yet what happens as you start to disconnect from fear is that you start to disconnect from your identification with who you are as an ego. The ego is your fear-based body that believes you are human.

You begin to connect with your light body, and in connecting with your light body, all of your gifts of spirit come in. You begin to become more vibration and less mass. You begin to leave your body in and out and in and out, and yes all these gifts of spirit, especially transporting yourself, will be seen in the next twenty to thirty years.

We are very excited for you, very, very excited…and those of you who are willing enough to be disciplined to do the ascension will see these good works of which we speak. Therefore, we say to you, as you do the ascension, we hear you say, "Yes," and we lower our frequency a bit and integrate with you as if walking in. With your "yes" and our "yes" there is agreement, and we lift higher. We lift higher in consciousness.

So, we have come from on high as guided by those who instruct us. You see, you are not the only ones taking instructions. There are more higher and higher gradients of light, higher and higher.

How far can you expand? It is for you to see, you know. But you will not know until you begin, so begin it and do the ascension exercise. Welcome this light I Am. Welcome this light into your aura and lift. And as you lift, feel love. Let yourself feel, feel, feel.

It is a precursor, the preamble of all that is to be on your glorious planet. There is much that is coming. This is a rebirth for you, this you have suggested to yourselves, the death of the ego, so the birth of the Christ itself is happening to your entire planet, and you are a part of it. You are mid-wifing the perfection of your planet by your willingness to show up, and we thank you for your willingness.

We thank you for this convergence of energy you have brought into this room, for you are making a difference every time you say, "Yes," and every time you choose to listen and act on the light I Am of your own spirit.

You are deities of light, and we love you. *You* are the beginning of Heaven on Earth. *You* are the beginning.

Now indeed, we will say to those of you who are listening, the next two weeks are very important. Much light is coming in, much, much light.

If you would include in your day, perhaps in the morning times of your day, lifting your heart and your arms up towards the sun and say, "Yes, feed me please the light I Am of higher consciousness. I Am love. I Am one with the true self. I Am the I Am, and I give great thanks for that, and that I Am aware of it. Help me to be all I can be, and I give thanks, and lift me please into the I Am now."

Let yourself be with that for 3 to 6 to 15 minutes. Hold that frequency and then we promise you, you will go altered throughout your day. You will be at a higher frequency, you will be more loving, more composed, more compassionate, and you will be less likely to respond with fear.

There is nothing to fear, but the ego is very seductive, and will find what you fear and will push that button, and that will be your opportunity, your grand warrior opportunity, to say, "Not me, I choose love, I choose light, I let go, I surrender, I am one with the light, all is well in my life, all is well in my world. I align, I identify with light of love I Am."

And then lift again. Lift immediately when you are challenged. Lift immediately when you are challenged and go back home and remember the divine experience of who you are, that you are the light of God and no less than that. You are the light of God. You are I Am consciousness in action, having a human experience, which can be transformed by your awareness of who you are.

Oh, beloveds, how we love you and how exciting is this time on Earth. We congratulate you for being here. We congratulate the courage and the trials you have been through. We congratulate you on your tears and your laughter. We congratulate you for showing up, and we thank you on bended knee from our hearts to yours.

We thank you for being here tonight so you could know it is going to be a shakeup. Things are going to happen—some laughter, some tears. You are going to build your own connection to spirit, and it starts right here, right now, this night. Listen. Listen to your connection to the I Am. Listen and act on that.

Trust this and trust your behavior when one with spirit. There is a higher knowledge, and it is in you and it is acting through you, and you have a great power in this small group. What seems to be modest in numbers is large in power. You are large in power. Unite in intention.

Let there be peace on Earth, let there be the greening of your planet, let there be abundance for all, let there be love for all, let there be food for all, let there be health for all, let there be joy for all.

You are on the verge of a grand transformation, and it is happening through you. It is happening through you, because you lived, because you cared, and because you chose love. Because you chose to surrender to love and not fear.

And so we thank you, beloveds, from our hearts to yours and back again, we thank you and your connection to the Almighty and to your roots, whether they be Egypt or Greece or Brazil or other.

You have roots on this planet and you have roots in the stars. Call your ancestors to you, gather your power, know who you are, and act on that. It is time. Anything other than that will bore you, we promise you. It is time. And so it is.

Be Bold in the Light
October 1, 2007

Indeed, my beautiful friends of light, know truly that it is I, Orion, here with you this evening, and the energy that calls itself Orion is powerful.

This evening, I break down the doors with you, and for you, and through you, according to your free will, as you call it, according to your invitation. For I see in this crowd, indeed, a gathering of great courage, and I see in this crowd, indeed, a gathering of those who are ready, of those who are willing to make great changes in their lives.

We see—for there are many of us in what you call the Orion energies and in who you have invited as angels and archangels—there is this in you ready for a change, and a change for, of course, the good, a change for the magnificent. We invite you to recognize once and for all who you are.

We have shared with you, indeed, that you are children of light. Let us share with you that you are creators of light, that which you are is light, is energy, and as you think, so you collect this energy. As you choose to feel, you collect more of this energy. And as you choose to focus, you collect more, until such time as you transform this frequency into a form.

So we are with you this evening as if tenfold energy is pouring down upon you to break down the door of your own resistance. We ask you, "What is this resistance?" Indeed it is fear of some sort. It could be fear that you do not want to hurt another person, because you are a good person, a kind person. You do not want to leave someone, perhaps, who has been good to you. But there is this that is calling you, like the wind it is calling you, and you must move on.

So, dear ones, we are with you, we are ready, and we offer to you this opportunity to simply say "Yes" to positive life change. We will then, as you in your individual minds choose to say, *Yes I am ready for something better. I am ready for more light, I am ready for boldness, I am ready for genius. I am ready not just, let us say, paying the bills. I am ready to experience Heaven on Earth, to have it all.*

Please remember, that which is God is love, creativity, wisdom and is you. It is nothing that is separate from you, and that is why we have come.

We who call ourselves the Orion energies come from a universe far away. We are like big brothers for you, and I, Orion, call myself father unto you. I will always be here for you. You, each one of you, may call upon me personally at any time. I am as if on call, and I will assist you. I will lift your frequency out of harm's way.

We are not talking about the third-dimensional world in which your body resides, in which your mind continues to convince you that you are human and that you reside in the third dimension. Oh no, we are speaking of something much faster. We are speaking of light, of light-encoded information that can change the frequency band of the physical. This is invited, this has been called, because it is time.

Have you but noticed there is some chaos upon your planet? Indeed. Not only country against country, but sometimes we see neighbor against neighbor, or family member against family member. Craziness all. And we remind you, it is just fear.

So as we come to you from this other universe, and it is not a universe that can be seen by any of your instrumentation, we bring purified, intensified frequency. We bring light gently, but very profoundly, into your energy field, into your aura, to assist you at the level of your willingness to open and heal.

What does it mean to open, and what does it mean to heal? Dear ones, beloveds, when you open, you begin to integrate more light, more frequency. What is going on on planet Earth at this time is that which you have been awaiting. It is ascension.

You have been sent angels, star beings, beings of light from many universes, and I, Orion, have come to collect my own. If you have been but drawn unto me, you are one of my own, and I love you. It is as a flock, for we know you know that word. We are family.

We would say to you quite certainly every one of you in this room is a star being, everyone in this room has lived many lifetimes, and every one of you in this room can relate to that which is being spoken.

And if you are willing, you can simply think to yourself: *I am willing to allow my light frequency to increase. I am willing to send up an antenna of light that I might harmonize with the Orion energies to begin to gather data to assist me in my joy as well as in my growth. I am ready for positive life change, and I am ready now.*

Dear one, the light I Am cannot harm you. The light I Am frees you.

Now, when this intense energy first comes in, it may not feel familiar. You are used to, let us say, drama, and that which is known as the ego is sometimes addicted to drama.

You have emotional addictions, you have physical addictions, and your mental addictions are your thought patterns you refuse to give up. We would suggest you review these. Are they serving you anymore? Is it time to let some of them go?

This light we are bringing into you this evening is tenfold, and much, much stronger than any other previous night, because you have grown and are ready, and because it is time for your Earth. So we bring in extra light to blow down this door of resistance in your life.

We are not necessarily here to save the planet, as it were, although this is a lovely thought and a lovely goal. We are here simply to tell you the truth, and you must save yourself, if that be your choice, if that be the way you choose to use your free will.

And yes, it will require that you choose to be willing, to be a little uncomfortable, because you will not be doing things the way you used to. People will look at you and wonder who you are, why there is so much boldness in you. But the boldness will come with compassion. It will not come with manipulation. It will not come with judgment. It will come with compassion, gentleness, meekness and understanding.

But it will be bold, and it will allow you to make changes where you will align with the integrity in your heart, not your mind, for your mind believes in the world. The world will die, but your heart will live forever.

So, we have come because the ascension is now. You might choose yourself as a savior in your own life. You do not need to save any other person. It is a good goal and it is a good thought, but you are here to save yourself, beloved, and that is enough.

Others will watch you, and if you are in integrity, they will be inspired. They will be inspired through your love and your gentleness, your integrity, your willingness, your compassion, your humility and your unity. They will fall in love with you, who you are, and what you have shown them as to who *they* are and who *they* want to be again. All you need to do is change yourself.

What would you change this evening if you could? What one fear would you give up if you could? What new thought would you embrace if you could? What new feeling would you choose to feel every day if you could?

You are a powerful being of light, creator god I Am, and you are loved. This is your opportunity to ascend into a higher frequency.

Whatever you have chosen in your life, whatever challenge, whatever difficulty, whatever fear, beloved, that is your key to your freedom. That is your door and that is your gift. Give God thanks for your challenge, because through your challenge lies your freedom. Through your accepting your challenge and overcoming it lies the freedom of the world.

You have been perfectly and gloriously made, and there are no mistakes. Whatever is happening to you right now has a higher purpose. Believe this, because it is true. Allow yourself to honor the God in you. Allow yourself to honor the light I Am in you. Allow yourself to recognize that *you* are savior in your own life. Stop waiting for the prince on the white horse. Look down and discover that you are sitting on the white horse. It is you. There is no one else coming.

When you say "Yes" to ascension, first you will find yourself happier. Secondly, you will find yourself not so worried about the chaos in the world, but you will recognize the peace within your heart. That is your home. And thirdly, you will begin to find, as you hang out in that beautiful heart of yours, you begin to change circumstance.

There is no person, place or thing in the world that has power over you, unless you give it power. If you feel you need to defend yourself when you are being attacked, resist not. When you resist, you are demonstrating fear or belief in another person's opinion. That is all it is.

An opinion is a thought of the mind. That shall die. That will end. But your heart will live forever.

Dear ones, teach them by holding fast to that which is eternal love and light and compassion. You do not need to change them or convince them. Just be yourself and love them. Let them be, and in letting them be, you are choosing love. And in choosing love, your frequency lifts and you join with the grand ascension.

There are many, many human beings on your Earth plane who are choosing ascension, who are choosing love, who are choosing non-judgment, who are choosing to show up for life and be a little uncomfortable for their passion, for their purpose.

Ask your higher self and your angel and any other spirit teacher you love to help you forgive yourself, to help you forgive anyone who has ever criticized you, anyone who has ever hurt you or harmed you, and bless them. Bless them in their ignorance and bless them because they, too, are children of light. They have just not grown into the recognition of that. They will. Then release them, and please release yourself and your past.

Dear ones, we thank you from our hearts to yours for following your path and staying on your path when your life has been difficult. You are honorable warriors of light. You are beloved. You are the light of the world. And for this, you have come to remember and to be who you are.

It is one thing to remember, very good to remember, but the next step is to be true to who you are. Please love yourself enough to have integrity, to honor yourself. When you really know who you are, you need no one's agreement.

Honor the God I Am within yourself and you are free. And that is all we ask of you. And then you are ascending. You are with us. Not only do we know, of course, you are with us, but *you* know that, too.

And that is the message we are trying to get across— that *you* know you are freedom, you are connected to beings of light, that we do commune with you, that you are loved, and that you can have the life of your dreams.

So, call upon us often, feel our presence. The more frequently you call upon us, the easier it becomes. We love you, and we are here to tell you Heaven is at hand right now.

Part IV

RESOURCES

Resources

Betsy-Morgan Coffman, representing the *Orion Technology for Learning to Channel,* is committed to providing highly qualified, gifted, and loving channels/teachers for the purpose of assisting humanity in achieving their highest ideals.

Our graduates work with individuals and groups in offering insight, psychic education, compassion, healing and awareness. All who graduate have the deepest respect for the integrity of this spiritual work and do it with gratitude and humility.

This is offered with the mission statement:

To serve the light by offering truth
with love from the higher realms.

If you would like to become certified as an Orion channel/psychic, or if you would like to work with a Certified Channel/Instructor, please visit our Web site at: www.AskBetsyMorgan.com/Resources.

How to Purchase the Ascension Exercise CD:

There is now a CD available giving to the listener a complete energy experience of ascension.

Betsy-Morgan channels Orion and offers an exercise which lovingly assists a person in lifting into their Light Body. This is done in such a way as to provide an educational tool for one to learn to do the ascension on their own.

The production of *"The Miracle CD"*—as it is called—creates the easy accessibility for a willing student of ascension to listen and enjoy this enlightening exercise on a daily basis.

"The Miracle CD" may be purchased at Betsy-Morgan's Web site: www.AskBetsyMorgan.com/products.